Seeing God Through the Tears

Seeing God Through the Tears

A Journey of Faith Through Grief and Suffering

MEL OQUENDO

WIPF & STOCK · Eugene, Oregon

SEEING GOD THROUGH THE TEARS
A Journey of Faith Through Grief and Suffering

Copyright © 2025 Mel Oquendo. All rights reserved. Except for brief quotations in critical publications or reviews, no part of this book may be reproduced in any manner without prior written permission from the publisher. Write: Permissions, Wipf and Stock Publishers, 199 W. 8th Ave., Suite 3, Eugene, OR 97401.

Wipf & Stock
An Imprint of Wipf and Stock Publishers
199 W. 8th Ave., Suite 3
Eugene, OR 97401

www.wipfandstock.com

PAPERBACK ISBN: 979-8-3852-3593-3
HARDCOVER ISBN: 979-8-3852-3594-0
EBOOK ISBN: 979-8-3852-3595-7

05/22/25

Unless otherwise noted, Scripture quotations are taken from the Holy Bible, New International Version®, NIV®. Copyright © 2011 by Biblica, Inc.™ Used by permission of Zondervan. All rights reserved worldwide. www.zondervan.com.

Scripture quotations marked NASB are taken from the (NASB®) New American Standard Bible®, copyright © 2020 by The Lockman Foundation. Used by permission. All rights reserved. lockman.org.

Scripture quotations marked NLT are taken from the *Holy Bible*, New Living Translation, copyright © 2015 by Tyndale House Foundation. Used by permission of Tyndale House Publishers, Inc., Carol Stream, Illinois 60188. All rights reserved.

Scripture quotations marked KJV are taken from the King James Version, which is in the public domain.

To my amazing wife: Jeanette, you somehow manage to keep up with all my wild ideas and boundless energy—I love you more than words can say.

To my kids: Soniely, Junior, Arianna, and Joshua, you are my heart and my drive. I'm so proud of the people you've become, and you inspire me every single day to keep pushing forward.

To my siblings, especially my kid brother Freddy: I've watched you grow into such an incredible man, father, and friend. I'm so proud of you, and I hope you know how much you mean to me.

To my granddaughter: There's nothing quite like the love between a grandfather and his princess. You have my whole heart.

Lastly, I dedicate this to the memory of Denise Gomez. To her beautiful children, Anthony, Edgar, Cristiano, Zekie, and my cousin Abraham: Denise's life was a blessing to us all, and her memory will forever live on in our hearts.

Contents

Acknowledgments	ix
Introduction: The Reality of Pain and Suffering	1
Chapter 1: Worship Amid Adversity	4
Chapter 2: The Poison of Unforgiveness	22
Chapter 3: Fighting the Right Enemy for the Wrong Motive	38
Chapter 4: Prayer Changes Everything	54
Chapter 5: The Silence of God in Our Suffering	71
Chapter 6: Why Do Bad Things Happen to Good People?	92
Chapter 7: The Need to Grieve	109
Chapter 8: Seeing God Through the Tears	126
About the Author	141
Bibliography	143

Acknowledgments

I WANT TO EXPRESS my deepest gratitude to those who made completing this book possible through their prayers, encouragement, and unwavering support. Margie and Greg Johnson—thank you for being vessels of God's love and support in my life. Your kindness has meant more to me than words can capture. Rick and Kimberly Thompson—your generosity and care have blessed our family in ways I could never fully express. Stephen and Emma White—thank you for always standing by me with steadfast support and encouragement.

To my cousins Freddy, Manny, and Micky Oquendo—this is what Oquendo love looks like! Your unique blend of love and strength, always there when I needed it, has been a source of pride and motivation.

Finally, a special thank you to my good friends Pastor Clint and Kelly Walker and Dr. Mark and Kim Andreson. Your friendship has been a true blessing.

Introduction: The Reality of Pain and Suffering

The Lord said, "I have indeed seen the misery of my people in Egypt. I have heard them crying out because of their slave drivers, and I am concerned about their suffering."

—Exodus 3:7

IN THE QUIET MOMENTS of despair, when words fail and our tears become our most honest expression, we confront the depths of our suffering. Pain, in its rawest form, often isolates us, leaving us feeling abandoned and helpless. This profound sense of isolation can create a chasm between us and our faith, making it difficult to perceive any divine presence or purpose in our suffering. Yet, within these intense moments of vulnerability, we are invited to seek a deeper understanding of our faith and connection to the divine.

Suffering is a universal experience. While it may feel deeply personal and unique, it connects us to a broader human condition. Theologians and scholars have long grappled with the nature of suffering and its place in the divine plan. In *The Problem of Pain*, C. S. Lewis asserts that suffering can serve as a catalyst for spiritual growth, challenging us to reconsider our relationship with God and our understanding of his purpose for our lives.

According to Lewis, pain has a way of piercing through the distractions of life, forcing us to confront our innermost beliefs and values.[1]

I know firsthand what suffering is all about. From witnessing my oldest son born with hydrocephalus and not living what many would consider a normal and pain-free life to experiencing the deep pain of infidelity and divorce, I have faced the harsh realities of pain, loss, and disappointment. These personal trials have tested my faith and deepened my understanding of God's role in our suffering. Through these experiences, I have realized that suffering, while deeply painful, can also be a pathway to a deeper connection with God.

In these moments of profound suffering, we are not merely left to navigate our pain alone. Exodus 3:7 offers a powerful reminder of God's awareness and compassion. The verse asserts that God sees the suffering of his people and is deeply concerned about their hardship. This divine awareness is not passive; it involves active engagement with human suffering and a commitment to address it. This perspective is echoed in the writings of several biblical scholars, who emphasizes that God's response to suffering is both empathetic and transformative, aimed at bringing relief and restoration.

The theological implications of Exod 3:7 extend beyond the historical context of the Israelites. It invites us to explore the nature of God's involvement in our personal suffering. This divine presence offers comfort and hope, reassuring us that we are not alone in our trials. The recognition that God is aware of and concerned about our suffering can serve as a profound source of strength and encouragement, urging us to maintain faith even when our circumstances seem overwhelmingly bleak.

Understanding that God is present in our suffering can transform how we experience and cope with pain. In *The Wounded Healer*, Henri Nouwen notes that our suffering can become a place of encounter with the divine if we approach it with openness and

---

1. Lewis, *Problem of Pain*, 97.

INTRODUCTION: THE REALITY OF PAIN AND SUFFERING

faith.[2] This perspective encourages us to see our pain not as a barrier to faith but as an opportunity for a deeper connection with God.

While suffering can feel isolating, it also invites us to seek a deeper understanding of our faith. Through the lens of Exod 3:7, we can find reassurance in the knowledge that God sees, hears, and cares about our suffering. This divine awareness encourages us to embrace our pain as part of our spiritual journey, finding comfort and hope in God's presence.

The movie *The Shack*, based on the best-selling book by William P. Young, features a poignant line spoken by the character Papa, portrayed by Octavia Spencer. In a powerful scene, Mack—played by Sam Worthington—confronts Papa, questioning why his little girl had to die. In response, Papa gently tells Mack, "When all you see is your pain, you lose sight of me."[3] This line encapsulates a profound truth: we must not let our pain blind us to God's enduring goodness.

Exodus 3:7 states, "The Lord said, 'I have indeed seen the misery of my people in Egypt. I have heard them crying out because of their slave drivers, and I am concerned about their suffering.'" This verse profoundly assures us that God is not distant or indifferent, even in our darkest hours. He sees our affliction, hears our cries, and is deeply concerned about our suffering. It reminds us that, despite the overwhelming nature of our pain, we are not forgotten. God is intimately aware of our struggles, and this awareness is the bedrock of our hope and perseverance.

I hope this book will serve as a companion and guide as you confront your own suffering and loss. Each chapter is designed to help you recognize and resist the tactics the enemy uses to lead you into a state of defeat.

---

2. Nouwen, *Wounded Healer*, 89.
3. Hazeldine, *Shack*, 53:00.

CHAPTER 1

Worship Amid Adversity

Naked I came from my mother's womb, and naked I will depart. The Lord gave and the Lord has taken away; may the name of the Lord be praised.

—Job 1:21

It was December 1999, and I was twenty-two years old, living in Ponce, Puerto Rico. At that time, I was already married (the reasons for my early marriage will be the subject of another book) and had a three-year-old daughter named Soniely, born in Chicago, Illinois. I had left Illinois and moved to Puerto Rico due to the hurt I experienced from my church and pastor back home. The church was a small, classic Pentecostal congregation where the approach to pastoral authority felt somewhat abusive. Having served as a youth leader and even starting to preach at sixteen, I found myself carrying deep wounds that bred rebellion. I no longer wanted to congregate, pray, or worship. Upon arriving in Puerto Rico, I struggled to find a nearby church, which made it all too easy to avoid attending any service.

As a result of my rebellious stage, I separated from my daughter's mother, a decision I made while still in Illinois. My hurt and anger so blinded me that nothing else mattered to me. During this separation, I received the news that I would be a father again, this time to a baby boy. It was then that I recalled a prophecy given to me a few years earlier in that small church I had once been a member of. The message was, "Says the Lord, you will have a son, and he will be special. He will be special to you and to all who meet him. I will use him; through him, you will become the man I have created you to be." I didn't remember this word until the day he was born.

On December 14, a sonogram was scheduled to ensure everything was going well with the baby and his mother. But things were not well. There was something incredibly abnormal with the baby that had not been detected in time. The baby had a condition known as hydrocephalus: "Hydrocephalus is the buildup of fluid in cavities called ventricles deep within the brain. The excess fluid increases the size of the ventricles and puts pressure on the brain."[1] This caused the baby's head to swell to the size of his torso. The cerebrospinal fluids had created so much pressure on his brain that the doctors were sure he would not survive. He was given only hours to live.

Amid personal suffering, whether it be the loss of a loved one, financial hardship, or emotional turmoil, it can be incredibly challenging to maintain a posture of worship. The natural inclination is often to withdraw, question the foundation of our faith, and struggle with the feeling that our worship is meaningless in the face of such profound pain. However, the story of Job provides a compelling example of how worship can persist even when everything seems to be falling apart.

Job's life, as detailed in the book of Job, offers a lens through which we can view our own experiences of suffering. Job was a man who faced unimaginable loss and adversity. Yet he maintained his integrity and worshiped God amid his trials. His story encourages us to reflect on our responses to suffering and consider how we might also choose to worship, even when it seems the hardest thing to do.

In Job's narrative, we see the importance of maintaining a faithful response to suffering. Even in the face of immense loss, his consistent worship practice teaches us that worship is not merely

---

1. Mayo Clinic, "Hydrocephalus," para. 1.

a response to favorable circumstances but a profound act of faith that transcends our immediate situation. It challenges us to consider how our worship can become a source of strength and connection with God, even when we are overwhelmed by the weight of our tears.

As we delve into this chapter, we will explore Job's story in greater depth, examining his devotion to God, the attacks on his livelihood, and his response to suffering. By reflecting on these aspects, we will uncover insights into maintaining our worship and finding God's presence amid our tears. This chapter aims to provide encouragement and practical guidance for navigating the complexities of suffering while holding fast to the hope and faith that sustain us.

Through the lens of Job's experiences and the assurance given in Exod 3:7, we will seek to understand how God's care and concern intersect with our own struggles and how we can continue to worship him even when our hearts are heavy and our spirits are weary.

The book of Job is one of the oldest texts in the Bible and offers profound insights into suffering and faith. While the exact author is unknown, some scholars suggest figures like Moses or Solomon due to their profound influence and deep understanding of spiritual matters.[2] Job's story is set in Uz, which is believed to be in the Edom region. This setting reflects a time similar to the era of Abraham, characterized by patriarchal customs and practices.[3]

Job's narrative stands out because it is set outside the usual context of Israelite history, speaking to everyone about the universal issues of suffering and divine justice. As John H. Walton points out, Job's role as a patriarchal priest and the cultural backdrop of Uz reflect the practices of the early patriarchs, helping us understand the broader message of the book.[4] This unique setting allows Job's story to address timeless and relevant themes to people from all walks of life.

2. Walton, *Job*, 23.
3. Walton, *Job*, 24.
4. Walton, *Job*, 24.

The book of Job invites us to explore the deep questions of why suffering occurs and how we can maintain our faith through trials. Job's experiences and his unwavering devotion to God, despite immense personal loss, resonate with our own struggles. His story serves as a beacon of hope, encouraging us to find strength and inspiration in our faith. By understanding the historical and cultural context of Job's story, we gain insights into how we can apply these lessons to our own lives and find comfort and guidance in our own challenges.

The Problem of Suffering

Job's story delves into the profound and perplexing issue of why a righteous person suffers. Many people wonder why bad things happen to good people, and this question has been a central concern in theological discussions for centuries. In his insightful work *The Problem of Pain*, C. S. Lewis explores this dilemma. He points out that suffering can shake our understanding of divine justice, leading us to question why a loving and all-powerful God allows pain and hardship. Lewis argues that while suffering is difficult to comprehend, it can also serve as a means to bring us closer to God. It challenges us to grow in our faith and trust, even when we cannot see the purpose behind our suffering.[5]

Job's story presents a major shift from the simplistic belief that all suffering is a direct consequence of sin. In fact, Job is described as a man who was "blameless" and "upright," yet he experienced immense suffering. His trials reveal that suffering is not a sign of God being angry with us or a result of personal failure. Instead, Job's narrative illustrates a more complex relationship between righteousness and suffering. His experience shows that suffering can be part of a broader divine plan beyond our immediate understanding.

The book of Job challenges us to reconsider our assumptions about suffering. It teaches us that being righteous does not exempt

---

5. Lewis, *Problem of Pain*, 38.

us from hardship or guarantee that we will be spared from trials. As Jesus reminds us in John 16:33, "In this world, you will have trouble. But take heart! I have overcome the world." Job's faith remained steadfast even when he could not make sense of his suffering, and this unwavering trust in God despite intense personal pain serves as a powerful example. His story encourages us to hold on to our faith, even when our circumstances seem unjust and our prayers appear unanswered.

By reflecting on Job's trials and his response to them, we gain a deeper understanding that suffering can have a purpose beyond our immediate grasp. Job's experience invites us to trust God's wisdom and seek meaning and growth through our struggles. It reassures us that our suffering does not diminish our righteousness or our value in God's eyes. It encourages us to find hope and strength in our faith, even when faced with the most challenging and painful situations.

The Sovereignty of God

The book of Job highlights the profound concept of God's sovereignty and wisdom. Throughout the narrative, we see that God is in control, even when life feels chaotic and unfair. A. W. Tozer describes God's sovereignty as his supreme authority over all creation, meaning that nothing happens outside his will or knowledge.[6] This idea can be challenging to grasp, especially when we face circumstances that seem unjust or when we don't understand why things happen the way they do. However, it also enlightens us, inspiring us to trust in his wisdom and sovereignty, even in the midst of our deepest struggles.

In the dialogues between Job and his friends, we're reminded of the vast difference between human understanding and God's infinite wisdom. Job's friends believed that his suffering must have been a direct result of some sin or wrongdoing, but the story shows us that this is not always the case. As the book of Isaiah puts it,

---

6. Tozer, *Knowledge of the Holy*, 109.

"For my thoughts are not your thoughts, neither are your ways my ways" (Isa 55:8). This doesn't mean that God is distant or uncaring; instead, it reassures us that we can trust in his divine control, even when life doesn't make sense. This trust in God's sovereignty brings a profound sense of comfort and security, knowing that we are under his loving and wise care.

Job's story also teaches us about the nature of God's governance over creation. It shows that God's plans and purposes often extend beyond our immediate understanding. In our lives, just as in Job's, we might face trials that seem arbitrary or excessive, but these experiences are part of a larger divine plan. By leaning into God's sovereignty, we learn to trust that he is actively involved in our lives, orchestrating events in ways that ultimately reflect his justice and mercy. This perspective helps us embrace faith even when our personal experiences challenge our understanding of a good and sovereign God.

The presence of the Holy Spirit plays a crucial role in our journey through suffering. The Holy Spirit offers comfort and strength, helping us to navigate challenging times with assurance. As the apostle Paul writes in Rom 8:26, the Holy Spirit intercedes for us with groanings too deep for words, mainly when we cannot express our pain or confusion. This divine assistance reminds us that God's sovereignty includes his active involvement in our personal struggles. By relying on the Holy Spirit, we can find reassurance and strength, trusting that God's plan is unfolding even when we cannot see the whole picture. Job's narrative encourages us to hold fast to our faith, trusting that God is sovereign and that his understanding far surpasses our own, even amid profound trials (Rom 8:28).

The Enemy Is After Your Worship

Chapter one of the book of Job provides a profound glimpse into Job's commitment to his family's spiritual well-being. Every morning, Job made arrangements to offer burnt sacrifices for each of his children, thinking, "Perhaps my children have sinned and cursed

God in their hearts." This was Job's regular custom (Job 1:5). This practice highlights Job's deep concern for ensuring that his family remained in right standing with God, even in their private thoughts.

An intriguing aspect of Job's story is the subtlety of Satan's initial attack. When Satan sought to test Job, he didn't begin by targeting Job's health or even his beloved children. Instead, the enemy's first move was to strike at Job's means of worship: his oxen and sheep. These animals were not merely sources of wealth or livelihood; they were central to Job's ability to sacrifice to God, a practice foundational to his spiritual life. By attacking these key resources, Satan aimed to sever the very connection that bound Job to God. The enemy's strategy was cunning—not just to inflict physical or emotional pain, but to undermine the spiritual practices that sustained Job's faith.

As the story unfolds, Job is confronted with a cascade of calamities. He loses his wealth, livestock, and, ultimately, his children. Each loss is a direct assault on his stability and resources, stripping away the elements of his life that supported his role as a devoted worshipper. The impact was profound as these resources were not only the means of his material security but also the instruments of his worship. The loss of these resources was a financial blow and a significant challenge to his faith. By attacking Job's ability to offer sacrifices, Satan sought to challenge his capacity to maintain his relationship with God. The true test was not merely in enduring physical suffering but in seeing if Job could continue to worship and trust God despite having his means of worship stripped away.

This aspect of the story highlights a deeper truth about the nature of spiritual warfare: the enemy often seeks to attack the obvious areas of vulnerability, like health or family, and the very practices and habits that sustain our spiritual lives. For Job, the loss of his oxen and sheep was more than just a financial blow; it was a calculated move to disrupt his worship and weaken his faith.

Similarly, when crises hit us—whether through loss, depression, or other forms of suffering—our first instinct is often to withdraw from the spiritual practices that once brought us comfort and strength. In times of deep pain, we might find ourselves reluctant to attend church, pray, sing to the Lord, or give financially. This withdrawal can feel like a necessary way to cope with the overwhelming weight of our emotions, as the very acts of worship that once connected us to God now seem too challenging to perform. The result is often a retreat into isolation where we struggle alone, cut off from the spiritual community and practices that could provide support and healing.

In her book *Grieving: A Beginner's Guide*, Jerusha Hull McCormack offers valuable insight into this experience. She highlights how grief can disrupt not only our emotional stability but also our spiritual routines. McCormack observes that grief often leads us to question God's goodness, causing a significant impact on our ability to engage in worship.[7] This disruption can create a deep sense of spiritual disorientation, where the familiar ways we once connected with God no longer seem accessible. McCormack's perspective helps us understand how crises can challenge the very foundation of our spiritual lives, making it essential to reflect on how we navigate our relationship with God during times of profound loss.

In these moments, it becomes crucial to recognize the importance of maintaining or redefining our spiritual practices. Rather than withdrawing entirely, we might seek new ways to connect with God that resonate with our current emotional state. Whether through simplified prayers, quiet reflection, or even just being in the presence of a supportive faith community, these small acts can help us maintain a connection with God, even when traditional forms of worship feel out of reach. McCormack's insights remind us that while grief and suffering may lead us to question and withdraw, they also offer an opportunity to deepen our faith by finding new expressions of worship that align with our journey through pain.

Moreover, Harold Kushner, in *When Bad Things Happen to Good People*, examines how profound suffering can impact our faith. He suggests that crises often force us to confront profound questions about our relationship with God and our understanding

---

7. McCormack, *Grieving*, 112.

of divine justice, leading us to reevaluate our beliefs and the nature of God's fairness.[8] Kushner's exploration underscores the notion that suffering can catalyze spiritual crisis, challenging our convictions about a benevolent and just God.

Similarly, Philip Yancey, in *Where Is God When It Hurts?*, addresses the dual nature of suffering in relation to faith. Yancey observes that while suffering can push us toward a deeper, more resilient faith, it can equally drive us away from it, creating a profound struggle to sense God's presence in the midst of pain.[9] This dichotomy highlights the critical tension between enduring faith and the temptation to withdraw, emphasizing the human struggle to maintain spiritual practices and trust in God during difficult times.

These insights from Kushner and Yancey emphasize the importance of continuing our spiritual practices and trust in God, even when faced with overwhelming circumstances. They provide a framework for understanding how crises can shake our spiritual foundations and offer guidance on navigating these challenges, reassuring us of the comfort and support that trust in God can bring.

Reflecting on my journey, I find a personal resonance with these perspectives. In that small church, where I experienced significant emotional pain, I was tempted to withdraw from worship and communal engagement. My aspirations to record music as a worship leader were met with strong opposition from my pastor, who refused to support my project and delivered a dismissive critique: "You do not have what it takes." This rejection was more than just a personal setback; it was a blow to my spiritual identity and sense of purpose. Feeling deeply hurt and rejected, I chose to leave the church, turning instead to secular music, where I sought and eventually found acceptance. This experience reflects the broader struggle described by Kushner and Yancey, illustrating how personal rejection and unmet aspirations can challenge our faith and prompt a reevaluation of our spiritual practices and beliefs.

---

8. Kushner, *When Bad Things Happen*, 45.
9. Yancey, *Where Is God*, 67.

Looking back, I realize that my immaturity profoundly influenced my reaction then. At just twenty-one years old, I was still in the early stages of my faith and life. Although my feelings were valid, the enemy used my pain to create a rift between me and my worship, leading me to distance myself from the spiritual practices that had once been so central to my life.

This personal narrative brings me to a pivotal moment related to the birth of my son Junior. The situation was dire: doctors had given him only a few hours to live. I vividly remember being taken to a room where a psychologist prepared me to meet my newborn son before his anticipated death. A neurosurgeon was also present to discuss his condition and answer any questions. They explained that Junior's head was abnormally large and would appear frightening to those unfamiliar with such conditions.

Entering the room where Junior lay in an incubator, surrounded by machines and cables, I was approached by a nurse who gently encouraged me to meet my son. She said, "Honey, go meet your son and touch him. He is beautiful because God made him beautiful." As I gazed at him, I was overwhelmed with shock and disbelief. The sight of my son in such a fragile state led me to question why God would punish him for my perceived wrongdoings. Why would an innocent baby boy be subjected to such suffering?

In that moment of profound despair, I experienced a supernatural encounter that shifted my perspective. The medical team had previously informed me that Junior was not responding—he had not cried, and they feared his lungs would not function properly due to the pressure from the fluids in his head affecting his brain. As I approached his incubator, it felt like everyone else in the room faded away, leaving only Junior and me. I heard an audible voice say, "You will have a son, and he will be special. He will be special to you and to all who meet him. I will use him; through him, you will become the man I have created you to be." These words echoed a prophetic message I had received years earlier but had long forgotten.

Overwhelmed by this encounter, I was compelled to recite Job's words: "Naked I came from my mother's womb, and naked I will depart. The Lord gave and the Lord has taken away; may the name of the Lord be praised" (Job 1:21). I fervently prayed, "God, forgive my rebellion. Please spare my son's life, and I will give you mine in return. I will serve you, do your will, and offer worship before you on behalf of my children until the day I die." As I touched Junior through the openings in the incubator and prayed over him, an unexpected static shock occurred. To everyone's astonishment, Junior opened his eyes and began to cry—something the doctors had not anticipated.

What began as a few hours of life turned into a few days, then months. Despite the doctors' grim predictions that he would not live beyond the age of five, my son, as of the release of this book, is now twenty-five years old. His life has been a testament to the faithfulness of God and the power of prayer. True to the promise I made in that hospital room, I have served the Lord in ministry ever since, dedicating my life to his service and continually offering my worship on behalf of my children. This journey has been one of profound challenges and immense blessings. Through it all, I have learned the importance of unwavering faith and the enduring presence of God, even in the most difficult of times.

Worship in the Midst of Loss

When tragedy struck, Job's first response was to worship. Job 1:20–22 tells us that after losing everything—his wealth, his servants, and his children—Job tore his robe, shaved his head, and fell to the ground in worship. He declared, "Naked I came from my mother's womb, and naked I shall return there. The Lord gave, and the Lord has taken away; blessed be the name of the Lord" (v. 21 NASB) This wasn't just a passive acceptance of his situation; it was an active, Spirit-filled declaration that no matter what happened, God was still worthy of praise.

In *The Message of the Psalms*, Walter Brueggemann emphasizes that "worship, particularly in the psalms of lament, becomes an act of defiance against despair." In the very act of worshiping amid suffering, he describes how believers boldly declare their trust in God's ultimate deliverance.[10] This is exactly what we see in Job—his worship was a Holy Spirit–driven response that defied the enemy's attempts to break him. It reminds us today that our worship is a weapon, a spiritual act of warfare that tears down strongholds and keeps us connected to the power of God even in our darkest hours.

Job's declaration in Job 13:15 (KJV), "Though he slay me, yet will I trust in him," reveals a faith that remains steadfast despite the circumstances. This isn't just a statement of belief; it's a profound expression of trust in God's character. Job understood that even when life is difficult, and God's ways are hard to understand, our response should be one of unwavering faith. This kind of faith is what many believers strive for—a faith that holds on to God's promises even in the midst of trials.

Worship is not just a ritual; it's a deeply personal and transformative experience. It's where we encounter God's presence in a tangible way. When we worship during times of loss, we're choosing to trust that God is with us, working behind the scenes even when we can't see it. Worship becomes a way to realign our hearts with God's will to reaffirm our belief that he is good and faithful, even in the midst of suffering. This transformative power of worship can empower us to face our trials with renewed strength and hope.

For those facing their own trials, the question arises: Will you let your pain pull you away from God, or will you draw closer to him in worship? Worship encourages us to press in during difficult times. It's about lifting our hearts to God, even when it's hard to find the words. It's about trusting that as we worship, God's presence will bring comfort and strength.

In these moments, practical steps can help maintain a worshipful spirit. Set aside time each day to connect with God, whether through prayer, reading Scripture, or simply being still in his presence. But remember, you are not alone in this journey. Seek out community support—friends or fellow believers who can pray with you and encourage you. Their support can be a source of strength and comfort. Engage in spiritual practices that keep your

10. Brueggemann, *Message of the Psalms*, 89.

faith alive, such as listening to worship music or journaling your thoughts and prayers.

Job's story, particularly his declaration in Job 13:15, reminds us that our faith is tested in times of trial. When we choose to worship in the midst of loss, we are not just enduring—we are finding strength in God's presence. We are standing firm in our faith, trusting that God is still in control and that he is worthy of our worship, no matter what we face. This enduring nature of faith can reassure us that we are not alone and that God's presence is a constant source of strength and comfort.

The Power of Worship in Trials

Psalm 56:8 offers a comforting assurance: "You keep track of all my sorrows. You have collected all my tears in your bottle. You have recorded each one in your book" (NLT). This verse reflects the profound truth that God is intimately aware of our suffering, capturing every tear we shed and holding them with care. It is a reminder that our pain does not go unnoticed by God, and every moment of sorrow is seen and remembered by him.

In *Real Worship*, Warren Wiersbe emphasizes that "Worship is not just an escape from reality; it is a confrontation with it. Through Worship, believers not only seek comfort but engage in spiritual warfare, claiming victory in God's promises despite their present pain."[11] This perspective highlights the dual role of worship in our lives. Worship is not merely a refuge from the hardships we face; it is also an active engagement with those hardships, an act of defiance against the despair that seeks to overwhelm us.

When we worship during trials, we invite God's presence into our situations, allowing his strength to become our own. Worship transforms our focus from the enormity of our problems to the greatness of our God. In these moments of worship, when we are most vulnerable, God's power is most evident. Our worship

---

11. Wiersbe, *Real Worship*, 47.

becomes a weapon, a declaration of trust in God's faithfulness, even when our circumstances suggest otherwise.

Worship is more than a ritual; it is a lifeline that connects us directly to God's power and presence. It is an expression of faith that says, "I trust You, God, even when I do not understand." Through this act of worship, we claim victory over our trials, not by our strength but by the power of the Holy Spirit working within us.

For those facing trials, Ps 56:8 serves as a poignant reminder that God is near, that he sees every tear and hears every cry. As we turn to him in worship, we can find the strength to endure, knowing that our worship is both a comfort and a powerful act of spiritual warfare. Through worship, we confront our reality with the truth of God's promises, allowing his presence to sustain us in every trial.

Seeing God Through the Tears

In the midst of our most difficult trials, it's often easy to feel that God is distant or uninvolved. We cry out in pain, sometimes unsure if he even hears us. Yet, it's in these moments of brokenness that we can encounter God in the most profound way, as Job did. After enduring unimaginable suffering, Job said, "My ears had heard of you, but now my eyes have seen you" (Job 42:5). His suffering wasn't just an experience of loss but a journey of deeper revelation—a movement from knowing about God to truly seeing him. This transformation, this journey from despair to divine encounter, is a beacon of hope for all of us in our own trials.

Through the tears, Job's vision of God transformed. At first, his knowledge of God had been based on what he'd been told, an intellectual understanding of who God was. But his suffering brought him face-to-face with the reality of God's presence. In the same way, our trials have the power to reveal God to us in ways we never anticipated. It is often in our darkest moments that God makes himself most visible—not because he was absent before, but because our pain opens our hearts to see him more clearly. And when we see God through the tears, our perspective changes, and worship naturally follows. Just as Job responded to his encounter with God by humbling himself in awe and reverence (Job 42:6), we, too, are drawn to worship when we truly behold God's presence amid our suffering. Worship, in these moments, becomes a powerful tool for deepening our faith and understanding of God's role in our lives.

When life is comfortable and easy, we can fall into the habit of relying on ourselves, listening to what we've heard about God without truly seeking to experience him personally. But when we encounter suffering, the noise of the world fades, and we are left with a choice: either turn away from God in bitterness or press into him in our need. It's in these moments of need that our personal relationship with God becomes most real, most tangible.

Seeing God through the tears means understanding that he is not distant from our pain. He is right there in the middle of it. The Bible reminds us that he is "close to the brokenhearted and saves those who are crushed in spirit" (Ps 34:18). As we bring our tears before him, God does not just observe from afar; he engages with us, showing us his faithfulness and mercy in ways we may have never fully grasped before. When we see God in this way, worship becomes the only fitting response—a recognition of his presence in the middle of our pain, offering us hope, comfort, and strength.

Just as Job's suffering led him to see God with new eyes, our tears can act as a lens, sharpening our spiritual vision. Through grief, we are forced to let go of our illusions of control and self-reliance. God reveals himself as the true source of comfort and strength in that vulnerability.

Consider how tears blur our physical sight, yet in that very moment, we often pause and reflect more deeply. Our tears force us to stop and pay attention. Similarly, in our spiritual lives, moments of pain make us pause, reflect, and see God in ways we might not when life is running smoothly. The tears, though painful, can clarify our understanding of God's character, his love, and his faithfulness. As our understanding deepens, worship becomes a natural outpouring—acknowledging God's power, sustaining presence, and unfailing goodness.

In our moments of deepest sorrow, when we feel weakest, we are most open to seeing God's strength. Paul wrote, "My grace is sufficient for you, for my power is made perfect in weakness" (2 Cor 12:9). In those moments of weakness, God's power becomes more visible in our lives. The tears we shed do not signify defeat but surrender—an invitation for God to step in and show himself mighty.

As Job's story teaches us, seeing God through the tears transforms our perspective. We move from knowing about God to truly experiencing him, from hearing with our ears to seeing with our eyes. As our perspective shifts, worship becomes the natural response to the majesty and nearness of God. Our suffering does not mean God has abandoned us; instead, it is an opportunity to deepen our relationship with him, to see his hand at work even when we do not fully understand the "why."

Application

Worship can profoundly sustain and uplift us during the most challenging times. As we've explored, worship is not just a ceremonial act but a vital connection to God's power and presence, especially when faced with trials. To harness the full potential of worship in your own life, consider these practical steps and reflective practices:

1. Create a personal worship space: Designate a quiet, comfortable space in your home where you can engage in worship and prayer. This space can be as simple as a corner with a chair and a Bible or as elaborate as a room with worship music and inspirational decor. The goal is to have a place that invites you to focus on God and allows you to experience his presence more intimately.

2. Keep a gratitude journal: Start a journal dedicated to recording your prayers, praises, and what you're thankful for. Regularly writing down moments of gratitude and God's faithfulness helps shift your focus from your problems to his

provision. Reflecting on these entries during difficult times can remind you of God's ongoing work in your life.

3. Incorporate worship into your daily routine: Find small ways to weave worship into your daily activities. Listen to worship music while commuting, use Scripture-based affirmations throughout the day, or take a few moments each day to pray or meditate on God's promises. These practices can keep your heart aligned with God's presence amid your busy schedule.

4. Seek community support: Surround yourself with fellow believers who can offer support and prayer. Join a small group or a prayer team where you can share your struggles and receive encouragement. Worshiping together can strengthen your faith and provide a sense of unity during times of hardship.

5. Engage in acts of service: Find opportunities to serve others, whether through volunteering, helping a neighbor, or participating in community outreach. Serving others extends God's love to those around you. It enables you to maintain a perspective of gratitude and purpose during your own trials.

Reflection Questions

1. How have you experienced God's presence in your life during difficult times? What specific moments of worship have brought you comfort or strength?

2. In what ways can you create a more intentional worship practice in your daily routine? How can you make space for worship in your busy life?

3. What practical steps can you take to maintain a worshipful attitude during ongoing struggles? Are there specific practices or rituals that resonate with you?

4. How can you involve others in your worship and spiritual journey?

5. In what ways can you seek or offer support within your community of faith?
6. Reflect on the role of gratitude in your life. How can keeping a gratitude journal or engaging in acts of service enhance your worship experience and perspective on trials?

Closing Prayer

Heavenly Father, we come before you with hearts both heavy and hopeful. In the midst of our trials and tears, we seek your presence, trusting in your promise to be near to the brokenhearted. Lord, help us see your hand guiding us through every storm and recognize your unchanging goodness even when our circumstances are challenging.

We ask for your strength to sustain us, knowing that our worship is a powerful declaration of our faith in your sovereignty. Teach us to use worship as a refuge and a weapon against despair, to lift our eyes from our troubles and focus on your greatness. May our hearts find solace in your presence and our souls be renewed by your Spirit. Guide us to create spaces of worship in our daily lives, keep our hearts open to your voice, and find comfort in the act of praising you. Help us to keep a spirit of gratitude, even when the path is unclear, and trust that you are at work in ways we may not yet understand.

As we navigate our personal struggles, let our worship be a testament to your faithfulness. Strengthen our resolve to remain steadfast in our praise, and may we always find you in our moments of need. In Jesus's name, we pray. Amen.

CHAPTER 2

The Poison of Unforgiveness

Blessed are the merciful, for they will be shown mercy.
—MATTHEW 5:7

Introduction

HAVE YOU EVER FACED a situation where forgiving someone felt utterly impossible? Imagine the profound struggle of extending forgiveness to someone who has committed severe acts against you or your loved ones—such as the killer of a child or spouse, or an abuser. The enormity of such pain often makes the concept of forgiveness challenging and seemingly unjust. In these situations, the idea of grace can appear to be an unfair alternative to the punishment that seems deserved. This chapter explores these intense struggles through the story of Jonah, revealing how divine mercy can conflict with our human sense of justice.

Jonah's reluctance to forgive Nineveh, a city infamous for its cruelty and oppression, is a compelling example of this internal conflict. His story highlights the broader implications of unforgiveness on our spiritual and emotional well-being. As we delve into Jonah's journey, we gain insights into the complex nature of grace and mercy, particularly when faced with extreme hurt.

Forgiveness expert Dr. Robert Enright, who discusses the psychological difficulty of forgiving severe transgressions in his book *Forgiveness Is a Choice*. Enright explains, "Forgiving someone who has caused deep harm, such as a rapist or the murderer of a loved one, involves not only a personal decision but also a profound emotional and psychological journey. This process requires acknowledging and working through the deep pain inflicted, which often feels nearly insurmountable."[1] Enright's work highlights the intense internal struggle faced when trying to forgive those who have caused profound personal trauma.

Additionally, Dr. Fred Luskin, author of *Forgive for Good*, addresses the practical challenges of forgiveness in extreme cases. Luskin states, "The road to forgiveness, especially in extreme violence or betrayal cases, often requires a transformative shift in understanding. It is not about excusing the wrong but finding a way to release the burden of anger and pain."[2] Luskin's perspective helps frame forgiveness as a process of personal liberation rather than an endorsement of the wrongdoing.

Understanding Jonah's battle with forgiveness provides a powerful lens through which to view our challenges in extending grace to those who have deeply wounded us. By examining his story alongside these expert insights, we can better navigate our struggles with mercy and justice.

Jonah's Call and Reluctance

Jonah's story vividly illustrates the intense internal conflict we experience when tasked with extending mercy to those we believe are undeserving. In Jonah 1:1–3 we read, "The word of the Lord came to Jonah son of Amittai: 'Go to the great city of Nineveh and preach against it, because its wickedness has come up before me.' But Jonah ran away from the Lord and headed for Tarshish."

---

1. Enright, *Forgiveness Is a Choice*, 54.
2. Luskin, *Forgive for Good*, 88.

Jonah's flight to Tarshish, a far-off destination from Nineveh in what is modern-day Spain, underscores his profound resistance to God's command. This resistance was not just an act of defiance but a reflection of his deep-seated belief that the Assyrians, who had brutally oppressed and conquered his people, were beyond redemption. The Assyrians were infamous for their cruelty, including severe punishments and torture, which had a direct impact on Jonah's community. This historical context makes Jonah's reluctance more understandable, revealing the personal and communal trauma that can cloud our ability to extend grace.

Jonah's struggle is a poignant reflection of a common human dilemma: the challenge of reconciling our innate sense of justice with the profound concept of divine mercy. This struggle, as articulated by theologian Miroslav Volf in his work on forgiveness, often stems from our inability to see beyond the immediate pain inflicted by those who have wronged us.[3] The severity of the wrongdoing, particularly in cases of extreme violence or personal betrayal, can intensify this struggle. For Jonah, the Assyrians' past atrocities created a formidable barrier that distorted his view of God's grace.

Furthermore, Jonah's experience underscores how deeply ingrained injustices and historical conflicts can shape our understanding of forgiveness. The weight of these cultural and historical grievances, as philosopher Martha Nussbaum notes, often makes the difficulty of forgiveness proportional to the perceived severity of the offense and the depth of the historical or personal wounds it has inflicted.[4]

Background on Jonah's Reluctance

The Assyrians were infamous for their extreme cruelty and violent methods of conquest, leaving an indelible mark on the ancient Near Eastern world. Historically, the Assyrians were known for

---

3. Volf, *Exclusion and Embrace*, 90.
4. Nussbaum, *Fragility of Goodness*, 45.

their ruthless military campaigns and systematic oppression of those they conquered. Their brutality was not only a tool for domination but also a method of instilling fear and submission in the populations they subdued. From flaying their enemies alive to impaling captives on spikes, the Assyrians made no effort to hide the terror they spread across their empire. This reputation for savagery became deeply ingrained in the collective memory of the people they oppressed, including the Israelites.

The Northern Kingdom of Israel fell to the Assyrian Empire in 722 BCE during the reign of Shalmaneser V and his successor, Sargon II. The Assyrians laid siege to Samaria, the capital of the Northern Kingdom, and they captured the city after three years. Thousands of Israelites were exiled, while others were left to suffer under the Assyrian yoke. Jonah, a prophet from this region, would have been acutely aware of the Assyrians' destruction, likely having witnessed or experienced their cruelty firsthand.

Given this context, Jonah's reluctance to obey God's call to preach repentance to Nineveh becomes more comprehensible. Nineveh was the capital of the Assyrian Empire and the center of its political and military power. Jonah's anger was not just a matter of personal prejudice but rooted in historical trauma. To him, the Assyrians were enemies who had caused unspeakable suffering to his people—people he loved, possibly even his own family. The idea that God would extend mercy to such people insulted Jonah's understanding of justice.

Psychologists and theologians alike have noted how deep-seated trauma and injustice can make forgiveness seem not only tricky but morally unacceptable. According to Lewis B. Smedes, "We are often unwilling to forgive when the offender has committed an offense so grievous that it calls into question the very fabric of our moral universe."[5] Jonah, bearing the weight of his nation's suffering, could not reconcile the idea of God's mercy being offered to such violent people.

This struggle is echoed by Miroslav Volf, who argues that the more heinous the offense, the harder it is to accept that the

---

5. Smedes, *Art of Forgiving*, 78.

offender is worthy of reconciliation: "Forgiveness flounders because I exclude the enemy from the community of humans and myself from the community of sinners."[6] Jonah's unwillingness to forgive reflects this very exclusion; he could not see the Assyrians as worthy of the same grace that he and his people hoped to receive from God.

The depth of Jonah's resentment mirrors the struggle many face when dealing with personal trauma. Whether in cases of national oppression or individual pain, such as forgiving a murderer, a rapist, or a perpetrator of extreme violence, the human heart grapples with the fairness of grace. Forgiving those who have caused immense harm feels like a betrayal of justice. However, Jonah's story challenges this way of thinking, urging us to confront the uncomfortable reality of God's boundless mercy.

The Assyrians were masters of psychological warfare, using terror as a means of maintaining control over their vast empire. Historical records, such as the Annals of Ashurbanipal, boast of the horrific acts committed during military campaigns, including mass executions, forced relocations, and the brutal suppression of uprisings. Archeological evidence from Assyrian palaces also displays reliefs depicting gruesome scenes of warfare, further reinforcing their reputation for cruelty.[7] These accounts illustrate the mindset of a people who viewed violence not only as a necessity but as an art form, cultivating fear and obedience through sheer brutality.

For a prophet like Jonah, hailing from a land ravaged by such a regime, preaching repentance to these people would have seemed unjust and a betrayal of his nation's suffering. Jonah's flight to Tarshish symbolizes more than disobedience—it represents his internal battle between justice and mercy, revenge and forgiveness. His decision to flee highlights the tension that arises when divine commands seem to conflict with human emotions and historical realities.

---

6. Volf, *Exclusion and Embrace*, 124.
7. Grayson, *Tiglath-Pileser I to Ashur-nasir-apli II*, 199.

Running from God's Call

Jonah's attempt to flee God's call reflects a common internal struggle when God's demands conflict with our sense of justice. Imagine his inner dialogue:

"You want me to do what? Preach a message of repentance? To warn them—give them a chance to turn from their wicked ways? To forgive them? No! I cannot, I will not. They don't deserve forgiveness. They deserve judgment to bear the full weight of their actions. They should be destroyed, not redeemed!"

Instead of obeying God's command to preach repentance to Nineveh, Jonah chose a path of defiance. He traveled to Joppa, an ancient Israelite port city, and boarded a ship bound for Tarshish. Tarshish, located in modern-day Spain, was known for its commerce and symbolic remoteness, representing the farthest point Jonah could imagine—he believed it was beyond God's reach. Jonah's flight wasn't just a physical escape; it was a spiritual act of resistance.

Jonah's choice to flee may seem too convenient—he found a ship, had just enough money for the fare, and the journey to Tarshish was as distant as possible. When we resist God's will, the enemy often presents seemingly easy escapes. This is a reminder that when we stray from God's calling, paths that lead us away from him can seem readily available and deceptively appealing.

We sometimes misinterpret these open doors as signs of God's leading, as Jonah might have thought: "Look at all these doors opening! A ship is ready, and I have enough for the fare—God must want me to go to Tarshish." However, not every open door is from God. As Scripture warns, "Satan himself masquerades as an angel of light" (2 Cor 11:14).

Jonah's flight is a vivid illustration of how we, too, run from God when faced with difficult commands. Like Jonah, we are often tempted to flee when God calls us to extend forgiveness to those we deem undeserving. It's easy to rationalize: "Why should I forgive them? They deserve punishment, not mercy." Just as Jonah found a ship to Tarshish, we often find ways to avoid God's will, convincing ourselves that avoiding the difficult task is the more justified path. But, as Jonah learned, running from God only leads to greater turmoil.

Proverbs 24:17–18 warns, "Do not gloat when your enemy falls; when they stumble, do not let your heart rejoice, or the Lord will see and disapprove and turn his wrath away from them." This passage challenges our natural inclination to rejoice in the downfall of those who hurt us. We often want to see wrongdoers punished, believing that justice requires retribution. But God's perspective on justice differs from ours. Where we desire swift judgment, God seeks restoration. His justice encompasses mercy, forgiveness, and the opportunity for repentance, even for those we consider unworthy.

The conflict between human justice and divine mercy is at the core of Jonah's story. Jonah wanted the Assyrians to be destroyed for their wickedness, but God wanted them to repent and be spared. This tension mirrors our own struggles when God calls us to forgive those who have wronged us. Jonah's resistance to God's mercy illustrates how difficult it can be to accept divine justice that extends grace to the very people we might want to see punished.

Proverbs reminds us that God's justice isn't about settling scores or indulging our desire for revenge. He sees the bigger picture—the potential for change and transformation that we often miss. God's justice is not just about what seems fair at the moment but about what leads to redemption. By aligning our sense of fairness with his will, God challenges us to rise above our desire for payback and trust his plan, even when it's difficult to understand. This emphasis on the transformative power of God's justice inspires hope and encourages us to embrace his bigger purposes.

This is where faith comes in. Forgiving those who have wronged us can feel like an affront to justice, especially when the wounds are deep. Yet, as believers, we are called to trust that God sees beyond our pain and anger. He is working out a justice that brings healing and redemption for us and those we struggle to forgive. The call to forgive isn't to minimize the harm done to us, but to release the desire for vengeance into God's hands, trusting that he will administer true justice in his way and in his time.

In aligning ourselves with God's justice, we reflect his heart. Just as Jonah had to come to terms with God's mercy toward Nineveh, we, too, are called to wrestle with our own feelings of hurt and anger and to offer grace to those who have wronged us—no matter how undeserving they may seem.

The Great Fish

Jonah's attempt to flee God's call took him aboard a ship bound for Tarshish, hoping to escape his divine assignment. However, running from God's will seldom leads to success. A violent storm arose, endangering the ship and its crew. Realizing that the storm was a consequence of his disobedience, Jonah took responsibility and instructed the sailors to throw him overboard. This moment serves as a powerful reminder: when we try to exact justice or take matters into our own hands, we often cause more harm to ourselves than to those we aim to punish.

As Jonah was cast into the raging sea, his situation seemed hopeless. Yet, instead of meeting a watery grave, God provided an extraordinary means of salvation: a great fish that swallowed Jonah whole. Jonah 1:17 recounts, "Now the Lord provided a huge fish to swallow Jonah, and Jonah was in the belly of the fish three days and three nights."

This miraculous event wasn't just about survival; it marked a crucial moment of introspection and transformation for Jonah. The belly of the fish serves as a metaphor for the times we find ourselves trapped by the consequences of our own choices, running from what God has called us to do. Like Jonah, we often find ourselves in dark and uncomfortable places, confronted with our resistance to God's will. These painful moments can provide opportunities for spiritual growth and transformation. They force us to confront our fears, disobedience, and need for God's grace.

Inside the fish, Jonah faced the consequences of his rebellion and began to acknowledge his need for divine mercy. In Jonah 2:2, 9 he prays, "In my distress I called to the Lord, and he answered me. . . . Salvation comes from the Lord." His time spent in the fish represented a profound death and rebirth—signifying a pivotal shift in Jonah's spiritual journey.

The belly of the fish became an unlikely sanctuary of grace. Though dark and confining, it was within this space that Jonah's heart softened and his perspective shifted. Having run from God's command, Jonah now understood that he could not escape God's will. More importantly, he realized that even in his disobedience, he was in need of divine mercy.

Jonah's time in the fish ultimately led him to repentance and obedience, reminding us that God's mercy is always within reach, no matter how far we try to run. God will go to great lengths to bring us back into his will.

God's Compassion vs. Jonah's Anger

After his transformative experience in the belly of the fish, Jonah ultimately obeyed God's command and went to Nineveh to deliver the message of repentance. Remarkably, the people of Nineveh heeded Jonah's warning. They turned from their evil ways, and their genuine repentance led to an extraordinary outcome: God relented from the destruction he had threatened. Jonah 3:10 recounts, "When God saw what they did and how they turned from their evil ways, he relented and did not bring on them the destruction he had threatened."

However, Jonah was enraged rather than rejoicing at the people's repentance. His anger reveals a profound struggle with the nature of divine mercy. Jonah's reaction underscores a common human challenge: grappling with the idea that God's grace extends even to those we believe are undeserving. Jonah's resentment stems from his deep-seated belief that the Assyrians, notorious for their cruelty and oppression, should not be recipients of God's compassion.

Jonah's struggle reflects a broader issue many face when dealing with the concept of grace. It is often difficult to accept that human standards of justice do not limit God's mercy. We find it challenging to reconcile the notion that forgiveness can be granted to individuals who have caused immense harm or suffering. Jonah's anger mirrors our potential frustrations when confronted with the idea that God's mercy surpasses our understanding of fairness. As theologian John H. Walton points out, "Jonah's reaction to Nineveh's repentance exemplifies the human difficulty in accepting divine mercy when it contradicts our sense of justice."[8]

In Jonah's case, his frustration is compounded by his personal history with the Assyrians. Their past actions against his people made it nearly impossible for him to accept their repentance and subsequent forgiveness. His anger highlights how personal grievances and historical injustices can cloud our perception of divine mercy. As biblical scholar Michael D. Coogan explains, "Jonah's anger serves as a stark reminder of how personal and communal histories can obstruct our ability to embrace the fullness of God's forgiveness."[9]

This confrontation with Jonah's anger provides a critical lesson for us. It challenges us to examine our attitudes toward forgiveness and grace. Are there individuals or groups we believe are beyond the reach of redemption? Jonah's story invites us to reflect on how we might limit our experience of God's grace by holding onto bitterness and resentment.

Ultimately, Jonah's reaction serves as a poignant reminder of the transformative power of God's compassion. It emphasizes that God's grace is not contingent upon our approval or understanding but is a testament to his boundless love and justice. As we confront our struggles with forgiveness, Jonah's story encourages us to align our sense of justice with God's infinite mercy.

Real-Life Example: Yiye Ávila's Forgiveness

The story of Yiye Ávila, an international evangelist from Puerto Rico responsible for evangelizing Latin America and often compared to Billy Graham, offers a profound and profoundly moving

---

8. Walton, *Jonah*, 87.
9. Coogan, *Old Testament*, 114.

example of radical forgiveness. Ávila, known for his powerful sermons on faith, healing, and repentance, was faced with an unimaginable personal tragedy: the murder of his beloved daughter, Noemí Ávila. The grief and pain he endured were immense, as any parent who has lost a child can attest. Yet, rather than succumbing to anger or the desire for vengeance, Ávila chose a path that few could even consider—he chose to forgive.

In an act that stunned many, Ávila visited the man responsible for his daughter's death in prison. His decision to meet with the murderer was not merely a gesture but a genuine offering of grace and reconciliation. Ávila's act of forgiveness, in the midst of profound personal pain and injustice, stands as an extraordinary testament to the depth of Christian mercy. It wasn't just surface-level forgiveness; Ávila extended the hand of fellowship and prayed for the man's salvation. He saw beyond the crime, beyond the hurt, and viewed the perpetrator as someone equally in need of God's mercy.[10]

This story, deeply rooted in Christian spirituality, vividly illustrates how God's grace can enable believers to transcend natural human instincts for retribution. Ávila's capacity to forgive reminds us of the kind of radical forgiveness Christ demonstrated on the cross when he said, "Father, forgive them, for they do not know what they are doing" (Luke 23:34). Ávila's faith allowed him to extend that same kind of grace, even in the face of such a grievous wrong.

Ávila's act of forgiveness serves as a powerful challenge to every believer. It asks us to reflect on the grudges, bitterness, and unforgiveness we might hold on to in our own lives. If Ávila could forgive the man who took the life of his daughter, how much more should we be willing to forgive those who wrong us in far less devastating ways? His story exemplifies the biblical mandate found in Col 3:13, "Bear with each other and forgive one another if any of you has a grievance against someone. Forgive as the Lord forgave you."

This extraordinary act of mercy did not come without sacrifice or inner turmoil. Still, it reveals the transformative power of

---

10. Created to Worship, "Yiye Avila—Testimonio."

God's grace at work in the life of a believer. Ávila's story compels us to look inward and consider how our unwillingness to forgive might hinder our spiritual growth. It challenges us to release the bonds of anger and resentment that can keep us from fully embracing the freedom that comes with forgiveness.

Ultimately, Yiye Ávila's story is not just about one man's extraordinary ability to forgive but about the boundless mercy that God calls all believers to demonstrate. His life and actions are a poignant reminder that the call to forgive is not conditional upon the severity of the offense. Instead, it is a reflection of the same grace that has been extended to us. Ávila's decision to forgive, despite unimaginable pain, is a testament to true forgiveness, not forgetting the offense but choosing mercy over judgment, love over hate, and grace over retaliation.

Trusting God's Justice and Mercy

God's justice is flawless, and he invites us to rest in his perfect way of administering it. Human emotions like anger, bitterness, and a desire for revenge can cloud our ability to see the beauty that surrounds us; they prevent us from seeing God. When these emotions take over, they prevent us from experiencing the peace and grace God intends for us. But when we relinquish the need to exact our own form of justice, we open our hearts to the beauty of God's righteousness and allow his justice to shine through. Our calling is not to seek vengeance but to show forgiveness and mercy, trusting that God's justice will prevail in its perfect time.

Romans 12:19 reminds us: "Do not take revenge, my dear friends, but leave room for God's wrath, for it is written: 'It is mine to avenge; I will repay,' says the Lord." This verse emphasizes the importance of stepping aside from our natural inclination to repay evil with evil. When we choose to trust in God's justice, we allow him to act according to his higher wisdom, which far surpasses our limited understanding. His justice, unlike ours, is both inevitable and perfect.

By trusting in God's justice, we free ourselves from the burdens of revenge and bitterness, making room for his mercy to be reflected in our lives. Mercy is central to God's character, and we are called to mirror that same grace in our interactions with others. When we focus on God's mercy, we can extend forgiveness even when it feels undeserved, reminding us of how freely God has forgiven us.

Micah 6:8 encapsulates this balance between justice and mercy: "He has shown you, O mortal, what is good. And what does the Lord require of you? To act justly, and to love mercy and to walk humbly with your God." This is not merely a suggestion but a clear directive to live in a way that reflects God's heart. Acting justly means treating others with fairness, while loving mercy goes further, urging us to show compassion and grace, even when it seems undeserved.

When we trust God's justice, we respond with humility rather than retaliation. Instead of allowing negative emotions to cloud our vision, we can see the beauty of his greater plan. This trust releases us from the chains of anger and bitterness, allowing us to experience the peace that comes from living in harmony with God's justice and mercy.

Conclusion

Jonah's story, paired with real-life examples like that of Yiye Ávila, illustrates the profound truth that God's mercy knows no limits and that his justice is far greater than our comprehension. We often struggle, as Jonah did, with the tension between wanting justice on our terms and recognizing the breadth of God's grace. Yet, the lesson is clear: God's compassion reaches even those we might deem unworthy, reminding us that forgiveness is central to his nature.

Forgiving those who have wronged us, especially when it feels undeserved, can be one of our hardest challenges. Jonah's anger at Nineveh's repentance mirrors our internal battles with bitterness, hurt, and a desire for revenge. But stories like Yiye Ávila's—offering forgiveness to the man who took his daughter's life—underscore how forgiveness, though difficult, reflects the very heart of the gospel. Ávila's choice to extend grace transformed a tragic situation into a powerful testimony of faith.[11]

Ultimately, we are called not only to receive God's mercy but also to extend it, trusting that his justice will prevail in his perfect timing. Forgiveness doesn't negate the need for justice. Still, it allows us to release the burden of vengeance and trust that God will handle all things according to his wisdom.[12]

Application

As we navigate our relationships and experiences, we must intentionally trust God's justice, rather than giving in to the desire for revenge. This choice requires conscious effort and a willingness to surrender our natural impulses. Instead of reacting to hurt with anger, we can seek to understand the situation through a lens of faith. Recognizing that God's justice is perfect and beyond our comprehension encourages us to release our grip on the need for personal retribution. By doing so, we open ourselves to transformation, making way for healing and reconciliation.

We can actively practice forgiveness by reflecting on our own experiences of grace and mercy from God. Each of us has been on the receiving end of divine mercy—an unearned and undeserved gift. By recalling these moments, we remind ourselves of the depth of God's love and forgiveness toward us, which equips us to extend the same grace to others. When we reflect on how God has forgiven our shortcomings, it becomes easier to forgive those who have wronged us. This act of remembering can soften our hearts and diminish any resentment we may hold.

Consider how we extend this same mercy to those who have wronged us. Forgiveness does not mean condoning the wrongs done to us; rather, it acknowledges the pain while choosing to release the burden of bitterness. We can reach out to those who have

---

11. Created to Worship, "Yiye Avila—Testimonio."
12. Walton, *Jonah*, 87.

hurt us, offering forgiveness as a pathway to restoring relationships or, at the very least, freeing ourselves from the weight of anger. Even small gestures, such as a kind word or a willingness to listen, can open doors to healing conversations.

Furthermore, we can participate in community conversations about justice and mercy, fostering an environment where healing and understanding take precedence over discord. This could involve arranging workshops or small groups centered on these topics, establishing safe spaces for individuals to share their experiences and challenges. By facilitating open discussions, we cultivate empathy and awareness within our communities, inspiring others to join us in embodying God's love and mercy. These conversations help us acknowledge our shared humanity and the universal need for forgiveness and understanding.

Take a moment to reflect on the people or situations where forgiveness is needed. Are there unresolved conflicts lingering in your heart? Pray and ask God to soften your heart, helping you see others through his eyes. This prayer invites the Holy Spirit to work within us, transforming our feelings of hurt and resentment into compassion and empathy. As we strive to view others as God sees them—flawed but worthy of love—we begin to understand the depth of their struggles and the reasons behind their actions. Trust that as you extend the mercy he has shown you, you will experience the peace that only comes from aligning with his will. This alignment fosters personal healing and allows us to be vessels of God's love in a world that desperately needs it.

Reflection Questions

- In what areas of your life do you find it challenging to trust in God's justice?
- How can you actively practice forgiveness toward someone who has wronged you?
- Reflect on a time when you experienced God's mercy. How can this shape your interactions with others?

- What steps can you take to align your actions with Mic 6:8, acting justly and loving mercy in your daily life?

Closing Prayer

Lord, we come before you with hearts full of gratitude for your unfailing mercy and abundant grace. Thank you for loving us even when we fall short and offering forgiveness when we least deserve it. Help us, Lord, to trust in your perfect justice, knowing that you see and understand all things. Teach us to release the need for revenge and extend the same compassion and grace that you so freely give us.

In moments of pain and anger, remind us of your love. Give us the strength to forgive those who have wronged us, even when it feels impossible. May we see your hand at work in every situation, trusting that you are bringing about your perfect will. And through our actions, may we realize the important role we play in reflecting your love and mercy to the world around us. We are your ambassadors, and we pray this in the mighty name of Jesus, our Savior. Amen.

CHAPTER 3

Fighting the Right Enemy for the Wrong Motive

Better a patient person than a warrior, one with self-control than one who takes a city.

—Proverbs 16:32

Introduction

Have you ever been so deeply wounded or betrayed that your response was driven more by anger than reason? This is a common human experience. Our emotions, especially pain and anger, often dictate our actions, leading us to make choices based on retaliation rather than righteousness. In moments of intense pain, it's easy to lose sight of what truly matters, allowing our hurt to cloud our judgment.

The Bible warns us about the dangers of acting out of anger. In Jas 1:19-20 we are reminded, "Everyone should be quick to listen, slow to speak and slow to become angry, because human anger does not produce the righteousness God desires." How often do we find ourselves fighting battles that seem just and necessary, yet our motives are misaligned with God's purpose? It is crucial to pause, reflect, and ensure that we don't get swept away by the moment, battling the right enemy for the wrong reasons. This internal conflict—between our emotional responses and divine purpose—is something we see clearly in Samson's life.

Samson's story vividly illustrates this struggle between divine calling and human frailty. Known for his extraordinary strength and infamous entanglement with Delilah, his story is often reduced to his moral failures. However, beneath this surface lies a deeper, more complex narrative. Samson's journey was not merely shaped by his physical might but by his emotional vulnerability. His life was marked by personal loss, betrayal, and unresolved anger, all of which clouded his judgment and diverted him from the mission God had set before him.

Rather than fully embracing his divine calling to deliver Israel from the Philistines, Samson allowed personal pain to dictate his actions. His obsession with vengeance and his impulsive decisions led him down a path of destruction, harming not only his enemies but also himself and those around him. In Judg 15:7, after being wronged, Samson declares, "Since you've acted like this, I swear that I won't stop until I get my revenge on you." While he was fighting the Philistines—the right enemy—his motives were often tainted by personal grievances, blurring the line between righteous justice and revenge.

The Bible cautions us against letting personal vendettas drive our actions. In Rom 12:19 Paul writes, "Do not take revenge, my dear friends, but leave room for God's wrath, for it is written: 'It is mine to avenge; I will repay,' says the Lord." Samson's story is a powerful reminder that even when we are called to fight for a just cause, our actions must be aligned with God's purpose. When driven by anger or the desire for revenge, we risk losing sight of our higher calling, just as Samson did. His life challenges us to examine our motives in the battles we face, ensuring that we act out of righteousness rather than retaliate.

As told in the book of Judges, Samson's life is a compelling narrative of great victories and significant flaws. Born with a unique calling to deliver Israel from the oppressive Philistines, he was endowed with immense strength to carry out his divine mission. However, as Prov 16:32 teaches, "Better a patient person than a warrior, one with self-control than one who takes a city." Samson's lack of self-control and his impulsive actions derailed his mission. The central lesson of his life emphasizes the importance of aligning our actions with God's purpose, a truth that resonates throughout his journey.

As we delve deeper into Samson's story, we see a man who often allowed his personal grievances and emotional turmoil to dictate his actions. Despite fighting the right enemy, his battles were frequently motivated by revenge rather than a commitment to God's will. This tendency led to unnecessary destruction and tragedy, derailing him from the divine mission he was called to fulfill.

Samson's life is a cautionary tale about the dangers of letting personal grievances take control, even when our cause is just. His journey challenges us to reflect on how easily our pain and frustrations distort our sense of justice. Ephesians 4:26–27 advises, "'In your anger do not sin': Do not let the sun go down while you are still angry, and do not give the devil a foothold." More importantly, Samson's story calls us to align our motives with God's purpose, ensuring that even in the midst of our struggles, we act in ways that reflect his will rather than our vendettas.

Samson's Calling and Strength

Samson's story begins with a divine proclamation in Judg 13:5: "You will become pregnant and have a son whose head is never to be touched by a razor because the boy is to be a Nazirite, dedicated to God from the womb. He will take the lead in delivering Israel from the hands of the Philistines." This verse highlights the extraordinary nature of Samson's birth and the divine purpose that accompanied it. Samson was not an ordinary individual; he was chosen from birth to be a Nazirite, set apart for a special mission. His immense strength, a gift from God, was intended to aid him in this crucial task of delivering Israel from its enemies.

FIGHTING THE RIGHT ENEMY FOR THE WRONG MOTIVE

Yet, despite this remarkable calling and divine empowerment, Samson's life often deviated from its intended path. Though sometimes aligned with his mission to combat the Philistines, his actions were frequently driven by personal grievances and impulsive reactions. In Judg 14:3, when his parents questioned his decision to marry a Philistine woman, Samson responded, "Get her for me. She's the right one for me." This decision led to a series of personal conflicts and violence that, while fulfilling his purpose of battling the Philistines, was not rooted in obedience to God's will.

Samson's life reflects a profound struggle between his high calling and the personal vendettas that clouded his judgment. His divine strength was meant to be used for Israel's liberation, but his personal anger and retaliatory actions often led him astray from his true purpose. For instance, Judg 15:7 shows his fixation on vengeance: "Since you've acted like this, I swear that I won't stop until I get my revenge on you." His retaliation, though directed at Israel's enemies, was often more about personal retribution than fulfilling God's mission.

Samson's life, with its unique purpose and extraordinary strength from God, serves as a powerful reminder of the importance of aligning our actions with God's will. In 1 Pet 4:10 it says, "Each of you should use whatever gift you have received to serve others, as faithful stewards of God's grace in its various forms." Samson's life demonstrates that having a divine purpose is not enough; we must ensure that our actions are driven by God's will and not by personal grievances or desires. Our divine gifts and callings are meant to serve a higher purpose, and we must ensure that our motives and actions reflect that commitment.

Samson's story serves as a powerful reminder that while we may be equipped with talents and callings from God, our journey involves more than merely fulfilling a role. It requires us to scrutinize and align our motives with God's divine purpose. Instead of allowing personal pain or anger to dictate our actions, we are called to act out of righteousness. As Rom 12:2 instructs, "Do not conform to the pattern of this world, but be transformed by the renewing of your mind. Then you will be able to test and approve what God's will is—his good, pleasing and perfect will." By doing so, we honor God's will and allow our divine callings to guide us in a manner that reflects his true purpose for our lives.

Samson's Anger and Revenge

What fueled Samson's anger? What event turned him into a man driven by rage and vengeance? The book of Judges vividly shows how Samson, a man destined for greatness, allowed his emotions to control him. It all began with a woman he was never meant to marry. Samson fell in love with a Philistine woman—someone outside of his people. This decision went against his divine calling. Despite the warnings, he pursued and married her.

The tension escalated when Samson proposed a riddle to the Philistines at his wedding, a wager they were determined not to lose. His wife, fearing for her family's safety after being threatened by the Philistines, tricked Samson into revealing the answer to the riddle and passed it on to the Philistines to avoid punishment. Samson, feeling betrayed by the very woman he loved, left to pay the debt he owed as a result of the lost wager.

However, his real heartbreak came when he returned to find that his wife had been given to another man—none other than his best man, a person he likely trusted deeply. Judges 15:2 recounts the father-in-law's explanation: "I was so sure you hated her," he said, "that I gave her to your companion." The betrayal was immense. To be wronged by the woman he loved and then to lose her to his best man would have cut deeply, stirring a dangerous mix of anger, grief, and shame.

But that was not the worst of it. In response to his outrage, Samson captured three hundred foxes, tied their tails together, set them ablaze, and released them into the Philistines' grain fields, vineyards, and olive groves, destroying their crops in a vengeful act (Judg 15:4–5). This act of vengeance escalated the conflict between Samson and the Philistines.

The final straw came in Judg 15:6 when the Philistines, in retaliation, burned Samson's wife and her father to death. The pain

FIGHTING THE RIGHT ENEMY FOR THE WRONG MOTIVE

and grief Samson must have felt are unimaginable. The woman he loved and her family were brutally murdered. How devastating it must have been for him to witness such loss, with anger boiling over as grief took hold. Experts on grief and trauma suggest that such profound loss often manifests as anger, particularly when the individual feels powerless to prevent the harm done to them or their loved ones. Dallas Willard, for instance, emphasizes the destructive power of unchecked anger in spiritual life, noting that unresolved pain can distort our perspective, leading to acts of vengeance rather than healing.[1] N. T. Wright further elaborates that when grief and pain are not processed through a lens of divine justice, they tend to result in actions driven by human retaliation rather than God's purpose.[2]

Samson, now driven by unchecked fury, lashed out once again. He struck the Philistines with great slaughter, killing many in a violent rampage. While his actions were directed at the right enemy—the Philistines—his motives had shifted from fulfilling his divine calling to pursuing personal vengeance. What should have been a mission of deliverance became one of personal revenge. His rage led him down a path of excessive destruction, far removed from God's purpose.

Samson's story illustrates the dangers of allowing anger and personal hurt to dictate our actions. Even when we are on the right side of a conflict, when our motives are clouded by bitterness and revenge, we risk inflicting more harm than good. Acting out of personal grievances rather than righteousness can escalate situations and cause unnecessary damage. Samson's life is a reminder to pause and reflect on whether our actions are motivated by God's will or by our unresolved pain. When we align our motives with God's purpose, we can pursue justice without allowing personal hurt to lead us astray.

---

1. Willard, *Renovation of the Heart*, 152.
2. Wright, *Evil and the Justice of God*, 36.

Real Life Story

In many ways, the emotional turmoil that fueled Samson's thirst for revenge mirrors real-world cases where unresolved grief, trauma, and the pressure to protect the family can drive individuals down destructive paths. A particularly compelling example is the story of Kevin, a quiet and studious young man, his brother Pete, a hyper and impulsive teenager, and their cousin Ryan, a troubled and aggressive teen with deep wounds of abandonment. Their lives were forever changed in 1993 when they became involved in the tragic murder of Kevin and Pete's abusive stepfather, Raul. Much like Samson, these young men acted out of a profound desire to protect their family, but that desire ultimately led to devastating consequences.

Kevin grew up in a close-knit family where loyalty was paramount. The values of protecting loved ones were deeply instilled in him, though he often felt overshadowed by his more impulsive brother, Pete, who had a history of gang involvement from a young age. Pete's understanding of family loyalty often manifested through violent actions. According to James Garbarino, children raised in environments where loyalty is intertwined with violence may internalize these values, leading to an increased propensity for aggressive behavior.[3] Their cousin, Ryan, added another layer of complexity. Abandoned by his mother at age two and raised by his grandmother until her death when he was eleven, Ryan experienced profound emotional neglect. Without stable parental guidance—his father struggled with alcohol and drug addiction—Ryan sought identity and belonging in the streets, embracing gang culture and violence as a way to fill the void left by his fractured family.

The trio's bond was cemented by shared pain and loyalty, but the boiling undercurrent of trauma would soon erupt. In 1993, Ryan, though still a minor of just sixteen years old, was fiercely protective of his family, including Kevin and Pete's mother, Sofia, who had long suffered under the abuse of her new husband, Raul. Sofia had divorced their father and pursued a relationship with

---

3. Garbarino, *Lost Boys*, 66.

FIGHTING THE RIGHT ENEMY FOR THE WRONG MOTIVE

Raul, who was many years her junior. Raul's abusive behavior toward Sofia was intolerable to her sons. The situation escalated when their sister Catalina revealed that Raul had also molested her and threatened further harm. Experts on domestic violence highlight that the presence of ongoing abuse can drive family members to extreme measures in an attempt to protect their loved ones.[4] The siblings felt compelled to protect their family, believing that family loyalty required them to act, even violently if necessary.

They decided to confront Raul and administer their own form of justice. In September of that year, Sofia asked Kevin to go to the apartment she shared with Raul to retrieve her microwave, purse, and television. At approximately 8:00 p.m., Kevin, Pete, Ryan, and a friend of Ryan's arrived at the apartment to collect the possessions and exact revenge on Raul. Along the way, they purchased duct tape to bind Raul. Ryan carried a knife, and Ryan's friend had a gun. All members of the group, except Kevin, expressed a desire to beat Raul. When the group arrived at the apartment, no one was home, so they entered and waited for Raul, who arrived within minutes. Upon his arrival, the group attacked Raul, beating him badly. To their surprise, Raul got back up and advanced toward them, which led to them stabbing him multiple times. In a moment of rage and fear, the gun went off, resulting in Raul's death. Judith Herman notes that acts of violence driven by emotional turmoil can quickly spiral out of control, leading to unintended and tragic outcomes.[5]

What began as a confrontation to defend Sofia spiraled tragically into a violent altercation. Kevin, typically more reserved and thoughtful, had never intended for things to escalate so far. However, like Samson, the trio was swept up in a collective fury of grief and a misplaced sense of justice. Samson's divine calling was often entangled with personal vendettas, and feelings of betrayal and personal pain drove his violent outbursts. Similarly, Kevin, Pete, and Ryan's actions were not solely motivated by a desire to protect their family but were deeply influenced by their unresolved

4. Dutton, *Domestic Assault of Women*, 134.
5. Herman, *Trauma and Recovery*, 120.

emotions. The consequences were devastating for both Samson and Kevin's family. In both stories, the initial intent—to protect loved ones—was overtaken by uncontrollable emotions, leading to catastrophic outcomes.

Samson's fury after being betrayed by the woman he loved mirrors Kevin's deep internal conflict during the murder of his stepfather. Both are cautionary tales, illustrating the danger of allowing unchecked anger and personal hurt to dictate actions. What began as a desire to safeguard their families ended in acts of destruction and personal ruin. These stories highlight how easily righteous intentions can be corrupted by personal vengeance and serve as warnings of the consequences of letting emotions—rather than wisdom—govern decisions.

The Dangers of Uncontrolled Anger

Ephesians 4:26–27 states, "'In your anger do not sin': Do not let the sun go down while you are still angry, and do not give the devil a foothold." This passage underscores the transformative power of managing our emotions, particularly anger, in a manner that aligns with God's will. The directive to not sin in our anger implies that feelings of anger are natural human responses; however, it also warns against allowing those feelings to dictate our actions. When anger is unchecked, it can easily lead to behaviors that conflict with our spiritual calling, resulting in decisions driven by bitterness or a desire for revenge rather than a pursuit of righteousness.

The latter part of the verse, which advises not to let the sun go down on our anger, highlights the importance of prompt conflict resolution. When anger lingers, it creates a breeding ground for resentment and negative thoughts, which can ultimately distort our perception of justice and righteousness. As the passage indicates, failing to address anger can give the devil a foothold in our lives, leading to further spiritual and relational damage. This caution serves as a reminder that we must actively work toward reconciliation with ourselves and others to prevent our emotions from spiraling into sinful actions.

FIGHTING THE RIGHT ENEMY FOR THE WRONG MOTIVE

In light of Samson's story, Eph 4:26–27 resonates profoundly. Samson, a figure from the Old Testament, was known for his great strength and his tragic downfall due to unchecked anger and a desire for revenge. Samson's unchecked anger and subsequent actions led him away from his divine calling, culminating in tragic consequences. Similarly, the story of Kevin, Pete, and Ryan reveals how unresolved anger and a desire for vengeance can lead to destructive outcomes.

Kevin, Pete, and Ryan grew up in a family where loyalty was paramount, instilling in them the deep values of protecting their loved ones. However, they eventually became swept up in a tumult of emotions. Driven by a desire to defend their family, their anger escalated, closing their eyes to the consequences of their actions. This story serves as a modern-day parallel to the cautionary tale of Samson. Ephesians 4:26–27 warns that when anger festers, it can distort our judgment and lead us down a path of sin—a harsh reality that Kevin and his family ultimately faced.

In the heat of the moment, Kevin and his companions resorted to violence, believing they were justified in their actions. Like Samson, whose fury blinded him to his divine calling, the young men acted out of collective rage that led to irreversible consequences. Their failure to address their anger healthily gave the devil a foothold in their lives, turning a desire for protection into an act of vengeance.

The parallels between Samson's story and Kevin's narrative serve as cautionary tales. Both illustrate the dangers of unchecked anger and the importance of resolving conflict constructively. Ephesians 4:26–27 calls believers to take responsibility for their feelings and ensure they align with God's purposes. By confronting anger in a healthy manner and seeking reconciliation, we can cultivate a spirit of peace and obedience that reflects our commitment to God's will. This approach enables us to engage in battles that uphold divine justice rather than personal vengeance, steering clear of the tragic paths that uncontrolled anger can lead us down.

Experts emphasize the significance of emotional regulation in maintaining healthy relationships and personal well-being.

According to psychologist John Gottman, recognizing and accepting our emotions is the first step toward managing them effectively. He suggests that individuals should validate their feelings while also seeking constructive ways to express them rather than allowing them to dictate impulsive actions.[6] Furthermore, Dr. Judith Orloff highlights the importance of acknowledging anger as a natural human emotion but warns that it should not be allowed to take control. She advocates for strategies such as mindfulness and communication to process feelings, suggesting that self-awareness can lead to more thoughtful and compassionate responses.[7]

Moreover, John Bradshaw stresses that understanding the roots of our emotions and taking responsibility for them is essential to overcoming anger and fostering true healing.[8] This comprehensive approach to emotional regulation aligns with the teachings of Eph 4:26–27, underscoring the need for believers to engage actively in their emotional lives, promoting healing and reconciliation instead of destruction.

The Consequences of Misplaced Motives

Samson's life reaches its tragic conclusion in Judg 16:21–30, where he performs his final act of strength—pulling down the pillars of the Philistine temple. His once immense power is used in a final, desperate bid for revenge, not for the liberation of Israel as initially intended. "Samson said, 'Let me die with the Philistines!' Then he pushed with all his might, and down came the temple on the rulers and all the people in it. Thus he killed many more when he died than while he lived" (Judg 16:30). This act, seemingly a victory, led to the death of many Philistines and Samson's own demise. His final moments demonstrate the devastating consequences of allowing emotions like anger and the desire for vengeance to overshadow the pursuit of God's will.

---

6. Gottman and DeClaire, *Relationship Cure*, 45.
7. Orloff, *Emotional Freedom*, 67.
8. Bradshaw, *Healing the Shame*, 78.

FIGHTING THE RIGHT ENEMY FOR THE WRONG MOTIVE

Samson's story is a powerful reminder that even those called by God can fall victim to misplaced motives. While his strength was a gift meant to deliver Israel, his misuse of it for personal revenge ended in tragedy. Throughout his life, Samson's actions were marked by impulsivity and driven by emotional pain. He sought retribution for personal slights, as seen when he destroyed the Philistines' fields in Judg 15:4–5, not necessarily because it was God's command but because of his desire for revenge. His final act was no different, underscoring the danger of allowing unchecked emotions to guide our actions. The very strength God gave him to fulfill a divine mission ultimately led to his destruction when used out of alignment with God's purpose.

This passage challenges us to reflect on the role of emotions in our spiritual walk. Anger, grief, and the desire for vengeance, while natural human reactions, can cloud our judgment and derail us from fulfilling God's will. Proverbs 16:32 emphasizes this truth: "Better a patient person than a warrior, one with self-control than one who takes a city." Samson's lack of self-control in his emotions led him to act like a warrior, but in doing so, he failed to conquer his inner turmoil. His strength, which should have been used to liberate Israel, was consumed by personal vendettas.[9]

Samson's life shows that the motives behind our actions matter just as much as the actions themselves. Although Samson's final act led to a victory over the Philistines, it was driven by his desire for revenge rather than a pursuit of justice or obedience to God's will. His motives were deeply personal, tied to the humiliation, pain, and anger he had experienced throughout his life. Ephesians 4:26–27 warns us, "'In your anger do not sin': Do not let the sun go down while you are still angry, and do not give the devil a foothold." When we allow anger to fester, as Samson did, it can lead to destructive decisions, even when we are fighting the right enemy.[10]

In the same way, our own actions—whether in our personal lives, ministry, or relationships—must be examined through the lens of God's purpose rather than personal emotion. It's easy to

---

9. Gottwald, *Tribes of Yahweh*, 89.
10. Wright, *Resurrection of the Son of God*, 36.

convince ourselves that we are fighting the right battles, but if our motives are rooted in pride, anger, or personal vengeance, we risk losing sight of the true purpose God has for us. As Jas 1:20 says, "Human anger does not produce the righteousness that God desires." Samson's story teaches us that our motivations should always be grounded in a desire to fulfill God's will, not in seeking retribution or satisfying personal grievances.[11]

Guarding against misplaced motives requires constant vigilance. We must be willing to pause, reflect, and examine the intentions behind our actions. Are we seeking justice, or are we acting out of bitterness? Are we pursuing God's will, or does personal hurt drive us? Proverbs 21:2 reminds us, "A person may think their own ways are right, but the Lord weighs the heart." It is not enough to simply engage in battles that seem righteous; we must ensure that our hearts are aligned with God's desires.

Samson's downfall came because he allowed personal grievances to outweigh his divine calling. Instead of focusing on the mission of delivering Israel, he became entangled in personal conflicts that led to his destruction. We must learn from Samson's mistakes by recognizing our misplaced motives and correcting them before we fall into the same traps. Doing so ensures that our actions serve a higher purpose, one rooted in obedience to God rather than being driven by personal emotions.[12]

The call to align our actions with God's will is a constant theme throughout Scripture. Colossians 3:17 instructs us, "And whatever you do, whether in word or deed, do it all in the name of the Lord Jesus, giving thanks to God the Father through him." This verse reminds us that everything we do, every battle we fight, must be done with God's purpose in mind, not our own. Samson's life could have been a testament to God's power and deliverance, but it was overshadowed by his inability to submit his emotions and desires to God's will.[13]

---

11. Willard, *Renovation of the Heart*, 152.
12. Dorsey, *Literary Structure*, 157; Gottwald, *Tribes of Yahweh*, 89.
13. Willard, *Renovation of the Heart*, 164.

As we navigate our own struggles and conflicts, let Samson's story remind us that God cares not only about what we do but also why we do it. Our actions, no matter how justified they may seem, must be aligned with his will. Only then can we experience the true victory that comes from living out our divine calling.

Conclusion

Samson's story underscores the importance of aligning our motives with God's will. While fighting the right enemy is crucial, pursuing this battle with the wrong motives can lead to unnecessary destruction and personal loss. Despite his strength and the victories he achieved, Samson's life ultimately reflects how unchecked emotions and personal vendettas can overshadow divine purposes, leading to one's downfall. His final act of vengeance, though significant in its scale, reveals the tragic consequences of pursuing personal retribution rather than aligning actions with God's true intent.

In the midst of our battles and pain, it is essential to remember that God remains present and attentive to our struggles. Even when circumstances seem dire and our emotions are overwhelming, God's presence provides a constant source of hope and guidance. We are invited to look beyond our immediate suffering and seek his direction. Doing so allows us to find the strength and clarity needed to act in accordance with his will rather than out of personal hurt.

Application

Examine Your Motives

Reflect on a recent decision or conflict you've faced. Were your actions driven by a desire for justice and alignment with God's will, or were they influenced by personal hurt or anger? How can you ensure that your future decisions align more with God's purpose?

Guard Your Heart

Samson's story reminds us of the importance of protecting our emotions from overtaking our purpose. What practices can you adopt to help you pause, reflect, and pray before acting on emotional impulses? How can these habits help you prevent anger or frustration from distorting your decisions?

Seek God's Will in Conflict

In moments of conflict or when facing difficult decisions, how do you typically discern God's will? What are practical ways you can invite God's guidance into your decision-making process, especially when emotions run high?

Pursue Justice Without Vengeance

Think of a situation where you felt wronged or experienced injustice. How can you pursue justice in that situation without allowing bitterness or the desire for personal vengeance to take control? How does Eph 4:26–27 influence your approach?

Reflection Questions

1. Personal vendettas vs. divine purpose: Samson's life was marked by personal vendettas. How do you think personal conflicts or emotional pain can cloud our ability to see God's greater purpose? Have there been times in your life when personal grievances took precedence over God's will?

2. God's purpose amid pain: Samson failed to fully embrace God's calling because of his emotional turmoil. How can we stay grounded in God's purpose, even when we're going through personal pain or grief? What biblical truths or verses help anchor you during challenging times?

3. Misplaced motives: Proverbs 21:2 reminds us that God weighs the heart. When you reflect on your own heart and actions, where do you see areas that need alignment with God's desires? How can you create space for God to reveal and transform those areas?

4. The power of self-control: Proverbs 16:32 highlights the value of self-control. Where do you see a need for greater self-control in your life, especially when it comes to managing emotions like anger or frustration? How can developing self-control positively impact your relationship with God and others?

Closing Prayer

Lord, as we close our time together, we humbly ask for your guidance in our lives. Help us fight the right battles with the right motives, seeking not our own desires but your divine will. Heal our wounds, both seen and unseen, and mend the brokenness within us that often clouds our judgment.

We recognize that our pain can lead us astray, causing us to act impulsively and out of anger. We ask for your grace to fill our hearts, transforming our hurt into compassion and understanding. Help us remember that our struggles do not define us; rather, how we respond to them does.

May we be instruments of your peace and justice in this world. Grant us the strength to stand firm in our convictions while maintaining a spirit of love and humility. Empower us to confront the injustices around us with wisdom and courage, bringing hope to those who feel lost or marginalized.

May the Holy Spirit guide us in every step. Let our actions reflect your light and love, and may we be beacons of hope in our communities. We pray that our lives will bear witness to your goodness and grace, drawing others closer to you. In Jesus's name, we pray. Amen.

CHAPTER 4

Prayer Changes Everything

Do not be anxious about anything, but in every situation, by prayer and petition, with thanksgiving, present your requests to God. And the peace of God, which transcends all understanding, will guard your hearts and your minds in Christ Jesus.

—Philippians 4:6–7

Introduction

When we encounter life-altering challenges—such as a terminal diagnosis, the collapse of a marriage, or the sudden loss of a loved one—the weight of these crises can feel overwhelming. Emotions like fear, anger, and despair surge within us, leading to questions about God's presence in our suffering. How we respond to such devastating news can significantly shape our spiritual journey. Will we allow the darkness of the situation to consume us, or will we choose to turn our gaze upward, seeking God's presence in the storm? Our reactions not only affect our mental and emotional states but also influence how we experience God's hand in our lives during these difficult times.

In moments of crisis, spiritual resilience becomes paramount. Kenneth Pargament notes that "people often turn to their faith to seek meaning, comfort, and control over their circumstances."[1] However, as we have seen in previous chapters, the enemy works against us to rob us of our worship, intimacy with God, and obedience to his will. This leads us to take matters into our own hands, distancing ourselves from the healing God desires for us. Our faith response—or lack thereof—can significantly influence the course of our healing and restoration.

In this chapter, we will explore the life of King Hezekiah of Judah, who faced a death sentence but responded not with resignation or bitterness, but with fervent prayer and unwavering faith. Hezekiah's story, found in 2 Kgs 20 and Isa 38, reveals profound truths about how we can approach our crises. His response to the seemingly insurmountable challenge of terminal illness offers a blueprint for engaging with God in the face of our most painful trials.

Whether confronting illness, the breakdown of a relationship, financial ruin, or the death of a dream, we can learn to approach our crises as Hezekiah did—with bold faith and unwavering hope that God hears our prayers and that his responses may surprise us in ways we never imagined.

King Hezekiah's Crisis

The story of King Hezekiah, found in both 2 Kgs 20 and Isa 38, offers a profound example of how faith can shape our response to a life-threatening crisis. Hezekiah ascended to the throne of Judah at the age of twenty-five and ruled for twenty-nine years during a tumultuous time in Israel's history. His reign was marked by a sharp contrast to many of the kings who preceded him, especially those of the Northern Kingdom of Israel and his father, King Ahaz.

Ahaz, Hezekiah's father, was notorious for leading Judah into idolatry and disobedience to God. He embraced the pagan practices of surrounding nations, even sacrificing his son in the fire (2 Kgs 16:3). Under his leadership, Judah experienced spiritual

---

1. Pargament, *Psychology of Religion and Coping*, 352.

decay, turning away from the worship of the Lord and descending further into practices that dishonored God. Ahaz's rule left Judah spiritually and politically vulnerable, and his failure to trust in the Lord led to alliances with foreign powers that ultimately weakened the kingdom.

In stark contrast, Hezekiah initiated sweeping religious reforms upon taking the throne, striving to restore the worship of Yahweh, the God of Israel. He reopened the temple doors, which had been neglected under Ahaz, and tore down the high places where people worshipped false gods (2 Kgs 18:4). One of his most significant actions was the destruction of the bronze serpent that Moses had made in the wilderness, which had become an object of idolatry. This bold move demonstrated Hezekiah's commitment to leading Judah back to true worship, free from idolatry.

Unlike many of Israel's kings, who perpetuated spiritual decline, Hezekiah stood out for his faithfulness. While the Northern Kingdom of Israel had fallen into exile under the Assyrian Empire during Hezekiah's reign due to persistent disobedience (2 Kgs 17), he witnessed the consequences of rejecting God's ways and was determined not to follow in their footsteps. The biblical record praises Hezekiah for his unparalleled devotion: "[He] trusted in the Lord, the God of Israel. There was no one like him among all the kings of Judah, either before him or after him" (2 Kgs 18:5). His leadership was defined by unwavering faith and a commitment to lead Judah according to God's commandments.

Despite his faithfulness, Hezekiah was not immune to personal suffering. At the height of his reign, he faced a severe illness that threatened his life. The prophet Isaiah delivered a devastating message: "Put your house in order, because you are going to die; you will not recover" (2 Kgs 20:1). This was a moment of crisis for Hezekiah. Having devoted his life to serving God and restoring Judah's covenant with the Lord, he was now confronted with death. This situation compels us to ponder a profound question: Why do bad things happen to good people?

In stark contrast to his father Ahaz, who turned to foreign gods in times of trouble, Hezekiah responded with faith and intercession. He immediately turned to the Lord in prayer: "Hezekiah turned his face to the wall and prayed to the Lord" (2 Kgs 20:2). This gesture was symbolic—Hezekiah turned away from distractions to focus entirely on God, seeking his intervention with sincerity.

Hezekiah's prayer was simple yet profound: "Remember, Lord, how I have walked before you faithfully and with wholehearted devotion and have done what is good in your eyes" (2 Kgs 20:3). His response was not one of anger or resignation, nor did he question why God would allow him to suffer. Instead, he humbly pleaded with God to remember his faithfulness. This moment of earnest intercession stands as a powerful example of how believers can respond to personal crises—not by succumbing to despair, but by approaching God with faith, trusting that he hears our prayers.

Hezekiah's Response: Prayer and Intercession

Rather than responding with anger, disillusionment, or passively accepting his fate, Hezekiah turned his face to the wall and prayed earnestly to God: "'Remember, Lord, how I have walked before you faithfully and with wholehearted devotion and have done what is good in your eyes.' And Hezekiah wept bitterly" (2 Kgs 20:2–3).

Have you ever wept bitterly? Hezekiah's act of weeping bitterly encapsulates a profound emotional response to his impending death, reflecting genuine despair and the weight of his circumstances. This intense display of sorrow highlights his fear of leaving his life and responsibilities behind and the depth of his faith as he earnestly seeks God's intervention. His tears signify a poignant recognition of mortality, prompting him to reflect on his life, relationships, and legacy. Moreover, they reveal a strong desire for healing and restoration. Hezekiah pleads with God to remember his faithfulness and commitment, hoping for more time to fulfill his divine purpose.

In the biblical context, this bitter weeping resonates with the tradition of lamentation, where expressing sorrow is not only legitimate but essential. As Ad Vingerhoets explains, "Crying can serve as a means of releasing pent-up emotions, providing a sense of relief."[2] Ultimately, Hezekiah's tears are a powerful reminder of the vulnerability inherent in the human experience, making his plea relatable to anyone who has faced similar trials and uncertainties. It's a reminder that even in our darkest moments, we are not alone in our feelings, and our prayers are heard.

This imagery illustrates a critical shift in focus. Hezekiah's prayer was not just a desperate cry but an awe-inspiring, intimate conversation with God, acknowledging his reliance on divine mercy. He called upon God's character—his compassion and grace—reminding him of his faithfulness and commitment to the covenant. It's a powerful testament to the transformative power of prayer and the depth of faith that Hezekiah possessed.

Hezekiah's heartfelt plea exemplifies the essence of intercessory prayer. He understood the importance of appealing to God's nature rather than merely listing his merits. By doing so, Hezekiah positioned himself as a humble supplicant, recognizing that his life was ultimately in God's hands. His bitter weeping signifies the depth of his anguish and desperation, resonating with anyone who has faced overwhelming grief or uncertainty.

As Mark Vroegop highlights in *Dark Clouds, Deep Mercy*, the act of lamenting and crying out to God is crucial in our spiritual journey. It allows us to express our pain and seek God's presence in times of sorrow.[3] Vroegop asserts that lament is not merely a passive expression of grief but an active engagement with God that can lead to healing and restoration. This reinforces the significance of Hezekiah's response: he chose to cry out to God rather than resign himself to despair.

Where Do We Turn When Things Get Difficult?

In moments of crisis, we often find ourselves at a crossroads, faced with the question of where to turn for support and guidance.

2. Vingerhoets, *Why Only Humans Weep*, 45.
3. Vroegop, *Dark Clouds, Deep Mercy*, 75.

Hezekiah's example demonstrates that the most transformative response is to turn toward God in prayer. His decision to cry out to the Lord when faced with death reflects a deep faith and trust in God's sovereignty, even in the face of overwhelming circumstances. This choice is not just a passive acceptance but an active pursuit of divine intervention. When the world feels chaotic and our circumstances seem impossible, seeking God's presence can provide the clarity and strength we desperately need. As the psalmist reminds us, "I lift up my eyes to the mountains—where does my help come from? My help comes from the Lord, the Maker of heaven and earth" (Ps 121:1-2).

In trials, we might instinctively look to other sources for comfort—friends, self-help strategies, or even forms of escapism like entertainment or distractions. While these alternatives can offer temporary relief, they often fall short of providing true solace and lasting hope. Ad Vingerhoets, in *Why Only Humans Weep*, notes that crying is a signal of "submission and helplessness," a deeply human response to crisis that calls for support beyond ourselves.[4] Yet, as Hezekiah's story illustrates, the greatest comfort comes when we turn to God. His peace, which surpasses all understanding, enters our troubled hearts when we relinquish control and trust him in our suffering. Turning to God, as Hezekiah did, invites a deeper encounter with the one who is able to provide not only emotional relief but also hope and restoration.

Personal Story: A Test of Faith in a Time of Crisis

In 1982, my father moved back to Chicago after separating from my mother. During this season of separation, which eventually led to their divorce, my aunts and uncles on my dad's side, who had been attending church, invited my mother to a small congregation in the mountains of Ponce, Puerto Rico, a community known as El Tuque. The church pastor was Eliel Cabá, and although my mother had not been particularly interested in church before or after this

---

4. Vingerhoets, *Why Only Humans Weep*, 45–46.

invitation, she accepted it, perhaps hoping it would ease her sorrows, and brought us along with her.

It was in that little church where my faith journey began. I was captivated by Bible stories, and my Sunday School teacher, who would years later become my stepmother, played a crucial role in sparking my interest. When possible, she would ask me to be her teacher's assistant for the day, seeing in me a deep interest that wasn't typical for most five-year-olds. In the short time we were at that church, I learned stories that shaped my life, like those of Samson, Balaam and the talking mule, and Jonah. She also taught me that all I needed was faith like a mustard seed, even giving me a tiny mustard seed to take home. I learned that when I prayed, all it took was a little faith for God to answer.

During this short period, my mom agreed to host a prayer service at the house, and many from the church came to pray. The pastor shared with my mother what he understood was a prophetic word: "The Lord tells me to let you know that he doesn't want you to go on the trip you're planning to Chicago. The Lord says, 'Death awaits.'" Despite this warning, my mother decided to go to Chicago, where my father had relocated. It's unclear if she was trying to start fresh or rekindle their relationship somehow.

This was the first time I traveled out of Puerto Rico. I was five years old, my brother Freddy was two years younger, and my sister Sandra had just been born. We stayed at my mom's cousin's house on the North Side of Chicago, at Wolcott and Division streets. One late afternoon, I was playing in front of the house on a Big Wheel I borrowed while the family was preparing for an all-white wedding. I was having so much fun. My mom sat on the steps, watching. My three-year-old brother started crying because I wouldn't give him a turn. My mom yelled at me, asking me to let him ride. I was upset because Freddy couldn't even reach the pedals.

Nonetheless, I got off so he could try. He didn't even know how to sit on it, so my mom yelled again for me to help him. I helped, maybe a little too roughly. I shoved him down in place. After about thirty seconds of sitting on the Big Wheel, Freddy started screaming loudly and desperately crying. I didn't understand what was happening—talk about a delayed reaction! But he wouldn't stop screaming. I saw my mom reach for her flip-flop and I knew what that meant. I started yelling, "It wasn't me! I didn't do it!"

My mother's cousin, Toñito, dressed in white and about to get into his car, rushed toward us with a pale face. I ran to hide, thinking he was going to grab me so Mom could spank me. Instead, he grabbed Freddy and rushed him to his car. My mom noticed that Toñito was now covered in blood, which was coming from Freddy's back. I went back to the Big Wheel and saw I was standing in a puddle of blood. My three-year-old brother had been hit by a stray bullet—a bullet fired by a Chicago police officer in self-defense after shooting back at a gang member.

My mom became hysterical. The other family members rushed to her side as she started to have a panic attack. Everyone was screaming. Some ran inside to call the police and an ambulance. All I could hear was my mom screaming, "They killed my baby! They killed my baby!" At five years old, I was in shock. I kept repeating over and over, "It wasn't me! I didn't do it!" Toñito's wife came to me, hugged me, and said, "You didn't do anything. It's not your fault."

At that moment, as my family reminds me, five-year-old Mel kneeled in the middle of the street, weeping as they drove off with Freddy in Toñito's car (the ambulance was taking too long), and prayed loudly, "God, don't take my little brother away. He's all I have." All I could remember was the lesson from Sunday School when my teacher said that if I had faith like a mustard seed, I could tell a mountain to move, and it would move (Matt 17:20). The family wept, not only because they thought Freddy would die but because they witnessed a five-year-old pleading to God for his brother. To this day, my family says they've never seen anyone pray with that much faith.

Freddy fought hard for his life. The bullet had perforated one of his lungs, and he had lost a lot of blood. His chances of survival were slim, and many began to lose hope. When my mom took me to visit him in the hospital, again I prayed, "God, don't take my brother away. He's the only thing I have." Somehow, my brother started to respond. He needed speech therapy to learn to talk and physical therapy to walk again, but God saw the tears and heard the prayer of a five-year-old. Today, Freddy is forty-five years old with three kids and two grandbabies.

I don't claim to have the gift of healing or to be a miracle worker. Yet, this experience profoundly reaffirmed the truth found in Jas 5:16: "The prayer of a righteous person is powerful and effective." That day, my childlike faith—my mustard-seed-sized belief that God could do the impossible—stood as a testament to the notion that genuine faith can wield immense power, no matter how small.

In moments of desperation, when the circumstances felt insurmountable, it was my simple yet fervent prayer that echoed through the chaos. As I knelt in the street, overwhelmed by fear for my brother's life, that mustard-seed-sized faith became my lifeline. I now understand that it was not about the magnitude of my faith or my ability to articulate a perfect prayer; it was about the sincerity of my heart and my willingness to trust in a God who hears and responds to the cries of his children.

This experience taught me that God is not looking for eloquent words or grand gestures. Instead, he desires an authentic relationship with us, where we can approach him with our doubts, fears, and hopes. It reinforced my belief that even the smallest act of faith can trigger divine intervention. I have come to realize that our cries, no matter how weak or fragile, are met with God's attention and love.

Through this ordeal, I learned that faith is not a static attribute; it is dynamic and often grows through trials. The miracle of my brother's survival was not solely a result of my faith but a manifestation of God's grace and mercy, revealing that he works through our vulnerable moments. It reminded me that when we cry out to God in faith, even with the tiniest spark of belief, he hears us and can move mountains on our behalf.

Ultimately, my brother's recovery was a powerful affirmation that God responds to the prayers of those who earnestly seek him, regardless of the perceived size of their faith. This realization encourages me to approach God with unwavering trust, knowing that even my mustard seed of faith can lead to miraculous outcomes. It serves as a reminder that no matter how dire our circumstances may be, we must continue to believe and pray, for our God is capable of the impossible.

Our Tears Don't Go Unnoticed

Hezekiah's prayerful response to his impending death is a powerful reminder that God sees and hears our tears. In 2 Kgs 20:4–5 we read, "Even before Isaiah had left the middle courtyard, the word of the Lord came to him, saying, 'Return and say to Hezekiah the leader of My people, "This is what the Lord, the God of your father David, says: 'I have heard your prayer, I have seen your tears; behold, I am going to heal you'"'" (NASB). God's response shows that Hezekiah's bitter weeping did not go unnoticed by God but instead moved him to intervene. Hezekiah's tears carried weight; they were not merely an expression of despair but a plea for God's attention and mercy that ultimately led to his miraculous healing.

Hezekiah's bitter weeping signifies a universal truth: our tears do not go unnoticed by God. In times of sorrow, it is easy to feel isolated and overlooked, wondering if our pain matters to anyone, let alone to God. Yet, Scripture repeatedly assures us that God is deeply aware of our pain and takes notice of our grief. The psalmist writes, "You keep track of all my sorrows. You have collected all my tears in your bottle. You have recorded each one in your book" (Ps 56:8 NLT). This vivid imagery emphasizes that God does not just witness our suffering from afar; he intimately values our tears, collecting and recording them, signifying that none of our grief is ever forgotten or dismissed. Our tears are precious to God, and every drop of sorrow that falls from our eyes has significance in his eyes.[5]

Tears are often seen as a sign of weakness in our world, something to be hidden or suppressed. Yet, in God's kingdom, tears

---

5. Vingerhoets, *Why Only Humans Weep*, 45–46.

are a form of prayer, a language that speaks volumes when words fail. Our tears can express what we cannot articulate—our deepest hurts, longings, and desires. They are a raw, unfiltered expression of our humanity, and God, in his infinite compassion, understands them fully. He responds to them not with judgment or indifference but with mercy and tenderness.[6]

When we cry out to God, we not only express our pain but also invite his compassion and mercy to flow into our lives. Just as Hezekiah's tears prompted divine intervention, our tears can serve as a catalyst for God's response. Through our honest expressions of sorrow and vulnerability, we create space for God's healing and renewal to manifest in ways that transcend our expectations. Hezekiah's experience shows us that God is not indifferent to human suffering but responds with mercy and action.

God's response to Hezekiah's tears reveals another important aspect of his character: his willingness to be moved by the cries of his people. He does not turn a blind eye to our suffering, nor does he demand that we "pull ourselves together" before approaching him. Instead, he invites us to come as we are, with our tears, fears, and brokenness, because he knows the depth of our pain even before we utter a word.[7] In Isa 25:8 we are assured of the future hope where God will wipe away every tear from our eyes, signifying his ultimate triumph over pain and sorrow.

Moreover, our tears are often a prelude to transformation. Just as Hezekiah's weeping led to his physical healing, our tears can lead to spiritual renewal and restoration. They soften our hearts, making us more receptive to God's work in our lives. In the midst of grief, it may feel like nothing will ever change, but often it is in those moments of deep vulnerability that God moves most powerfully. The Bible reminds us, "Those who sow with tears will reap with songs of joy" (Ps 126:5). Tears are not wasted; they are seeds that when sown in faith, yield a harvest of healing, hope, and joy.[8]

---

6. Vroegop, *Dark Clouds, Deep Mercy*, 75.
7. Willard, *Divine Conspiracy*, 152.
8. Wright, *Evil and the Justice of God*, 36.

This doesn't mean that every tear is instantly followed by a miraculous healing or immediate relief from suffering, as we might hope. But it does mean that God is present in the process. He is with us in our pain, working behind the scenes in ways we cannot yet see. Just as Hezekiah had to trust God in his moment of despair, we, too, are called to trust that God is faithful and will respond to our cries in his perfect timing and according to his divine wisdom.

In our darkest moments, when it feels like no one sees our pain, we can take comfort in knowing that God not only sees, but he cares deeply. He collects every tear and responds to our heartache with compassion and love. Whether our tears come from loss, fear, or brokenness, we can rest assured that none of them go unnoticed by the one who holds the power to heal, restore, and bring hope into our live

Four Key Truths We Can Draw from Hezekiah's Story

1. *Our tears don't go unnoticed*: God is fully aware of every tear we shed. He sees our distress and hears our cries, even when we feel isolated in our suffering. Hezekiah's story demonstrates that God is present in our pain, attentive to our deepest sorrows.

2. *Remember that God remembers*: Hezekiah reminded God of his faithfulness, and God responded. This act underscores that God does not forget his people or their devotion. We can take heart in knowing that God remembers his promises and our acts of faith, affirming his covenant and his justice.

3. *You can see God through your tears*: In the midst of suffering, it can be difficult to perceive God's presence. Yet, Hezekiah's story reminds us that even when circumstances seem bleak, God is with us, seeing our pain and ready to act on our behalf. Our tears are not obstacles to seeing God, but rather,

they can draw us closer to him, allowing us to experience his healing presence.

4. *The prayer of the righteous moves the heart of God*: Hezekiah's heartfelt prayer led to a dramatic reversal of his circumstances. His example reminds us that the prayers of those who seek God with a pure heart are potent and effective, capable of moving God's heart and hand. Prayer, when offered in faith, is powerful and can change the course of events.

Hezekiah's tears, and the response they evoked, remind us that in our moments of greatest vulnerability, God is present, aware, and responsive. Our tears are not wasted; they are seen by the One who holds all power to heal and restore. In our suffering, he answers with compassion, grace, and divine intervention.

The Power of Prayer

Hezekiah's story is a profound testament to the significance of prayer during times of crisis. Faced with the devastating news from the prophet Isaiah that he would soon die, Hezekiah turned to God with heartfelt supplication. This act of seeking divine help underscores a crucial truth: sincere prayer can pave the way for divine intervention. As Jas 5:16 affirms, "The prayer of a righteous person is powerful and effective." Hezekiah's earnest plea illustrates how prayer, grounded in faith, can profoundly shape our circumstances.

In my own life, this truth became strikingly real when, at the age of five, I knelt in the middle of the street, crying out to God for my younger brother's life after he was accidentally shot. Just as Hezekiah's prayers brought about miraculous intervention, my desperate plea for Freddy became a vital cry for divine healing. The memory of that moment remains etched in my heart; I can still feel the intensity of my desperation and the unwavering hope that my cries would reach the heavens.

Scholars have noted that prayer is not merely a means of seeking assistance; it serves as an acknowledgment of our dependence on God and an expression of faith in his ability to act. In his book *Prayer: Finding the Heart's True Home*, Richard Foster emphasizes prayer as a deep, relational experience that fosters intimacy with God.[9] This perspective resonates with my experience; prayer became my lifeline during moments of profound need—a way to connect deeply with God.

Moreover, prayer serves as a powerful reminder of our vulnerability. In times of trouble, we often realize we cannot rely solely on our strength or understanding. Hezekiah's prayer was not a last resort but a first response—a proactive measure that acknowledged the gravity of his situation while simultaneously placing trust in God's sovereignty. In *Prayer: Experiencing Awe and Intimacy with God*, Timothy Keller notes that prayer invites us to express our fears and hopes to God, fostering a sense of divine presence that reassures us in our trials.[10]

Reflecting on my own life experiences, as hard as they may be, I always feel an overwhelming sense of peace that washes over me. I can feel God's presence surrounding me, providing comfort amid the chaos. This aligns with the understanding that prayer is not solely about requesting help but also about cultivating a deeper relationship with God built on trust and intimacy. Prayer creates a sacred space where we can lay our burdens before him, confident that he cares for us deeply.

Prayer has the transformative power to change our circumstances and ourselves. It shapes our character, helping us to grow in patience, humility, and faith. When we commit our challenges to God in prayer, we view our situations through his eyes, cultivating a sense of hope and resilience. In *Simply Jesus*, N. T. Wright suggests that prayer positions us to receive God's transformative power, allowing us to become instruments of his will on earth.[11]

In essence, the power of prayer is multifaceted. It serves as a vehicle for divine intervention, a means of expressing vulnerability, and a pathway toward personal transformation. Like Hezekiah,

---

9. Foster, *Prayer*, 34.
10. Keller, *Prayer*, 98.
11. Wright, *Simply Jesus*, 75.

we are invited to approach God boldly, trusting that our prayers can move mountains. As we navigate life's challenges, may we remember the invaluable lessons from Hezekiah's example, allowing our faith-filled prayers to shape our circumstances and draw us closer to God's heart.

The stories of Hezekiah and my own experience illustrate the profound impact of prayer. Let us embrace prayer as a vital aspect of our lives, recognizing its power to change our hearts, influence our circumstances, and foster a deeper connection with God. In doing so, we can cultivate a life of resilient faith in the face of adversity and rich in divine intimacy.

Conclusion

King Hezekiah's response to his crisis offers a compelling model for approaching our own challenges. His example teaches us the power of prayer and the importance of interceding with faith and sincerity. In the face of a terminal diagnosis, Hezekiah did not turn away from God or become resigned to his fate. Instead, he brought his pain, fears, and deepest desires before God with an open heart, trusting in his compassion. His story reminds us that God sees and hears us in our moments of greatest need and that earnest, faith-filled prayers can move the heart of God to intervene.

The lesson is clear: when we face devastating news or profound challenges, we are called to turn to God with the same earnestness and faith. Hezekiah's prayer wasn't just about prolonging his life; it was a plea for God's mercy and a recognition that the situation was beyond his control. Likewise, our prayers invite God into the darkest corners of our lives, trusting him to work in ways we cannot predict. Whether God's intervention is immediate or unfolds over time, our posture in prayer should reflect trust, surrender, and hope in his ability to act. Hezekiah's story encourages us to believe that no matter the severity of our circumstances, God is always present and willing to hear the cries of his people.

Application

Take a moment to reflect on how you have responded to personal crises in your own life. Have there been moments when fear, anger, or despair overshadowed your faith? It is easy, in the face of difficult news or overwhelming challenges, to react with hopelessness or even resignation, believing that our situation is beyond change. But Hezekiah's story shows us a different path. How can you begin incorporating Hezekiah's approach into your future responses to crises? Reflecting on our past responses can help us grow and develop a more faith-filled approach to future challenges.

Consider the role of prayer in your life—particularly in times of hardship. Have you brought your full heart to God, asking for his help with the faith that he not only hears you but also cares deeply for you? Or have you hesitated, assuming your situation was unchangeable? Challenge yourself to commit to seeking God's will through persistent prayer and intercession in your times of trouble. Remember, prayer is not just a means of asking for help but a way to align our will with God's and to seek his guidance and comfort in our times of need. As you go forward, remember that God desires to meet you in your brokenness, and he is faithful to respond in ways that will ultimately lead to healing and growth, even if it is not always in the way we expect.

Reflection Questions

1. How do you personally acknowledge your vulnerabilities when facing crises? In what ways can you express these feelings to God in prayer, following Hezekiah's example?

2. Reflect on a time when your prayers seemed to change your circumstances, whether positively or negatively. How did this experience shape your understanding of prayer's power and effectiveness?

3. How has your perspective on God's presence during suffering evolved over time? Can you identify moments where your pain led you to a deeper understanding of his love and faithfulness?

4. Hezekiah reminded God of his faithfulness. How can you incorporate reminders of God's past faithfulness in your own life? What scriptures, stories, or personal experiences can you recall to strengthen your faith during difficult times?

5. In your current life situation, what specific areas do you feel called to bring before God in prayer? How can you align your requests with faith in his sovereignty and goodness, trusting that he hears and responds to your needs?

Closing Prayer

Lord, we come to you with our burdens and fears, just as Hezekiah did. When we feel overwhelmed by crisis, help us remember that you are near, ready to hear and respond to our cries. Teach us to approach you with honest and earnest prayers, trusting not in our own strength but in your power and compassion. Guide us through the storms of life, and may we find hope and strength in your presence. Transform our despair into faith, our anger into peace, and our fears into hope. Let your will be done in our lives as we rest in the assurance that you are always with us, working for our good. In Jesus's name, we pray. Amen.

CHAPTER 5

The Silence of God in Our Suffering

How long, Lord? Will you forget me forever? How long will you hide your face from me? How long must I wrestle with my thoughts and day after day have sorrow in my heart?

—Psalm 13:1–2

Introduction

IN MOMENTS OF PROFOUND anguish, when the pain of our trauma or the reality of our loss intensifies, time seems to slow down. We are left alone with the raw ache of unanswered questions, grappling with the haunting query: Where is God when I need him the most? This inquiry is not casual; it is a cry that reverberates from the deepest recesses of the soul, born out of desperation, especially after pouring our hearts out in prayer, only to be met with silence.

Such silence can feel suffocating, leaving us to wonder if our prayers ever reached the heavens. For many, these moments are marked by a sense of betrayal. We pray fervently for healing, yet illness claims our loved ones; we plead for peace in our hearts, but the storm of grief rages on. This struggle is intensely personal yet universally shared, whether through a marriage dissolving despite fervent prayers for reconciliation or a parent's worst fear realized when a child is lost. These experiences can shake the very foundations of our faith, compelling us to confront the pain of loss and the disorienting reality of seemingly unanswered prayers.

As C. S. Lewis states, "Pain insists upon being attended to. God whispers to us in our pleasures, speaks in our consciences, but shouts in our pains: it is His megaphone to rouse a deaf world."[1] However, unlike the account of King Hezekiah, who witnessed God miraculously extend his life, this chapter confronts the painful reality of unanswered prayers. What happens when we cry out to God in our most profound moments of need, pleading for healing, restoration, or deliverance, only to feel abandoned in our suffering?

In exploring these profound questions through the lens of personal loss and grief, we will engage with real-life stories that reflect the heart-wrenching experiences of those who have prayed for miracles yet faced despair instead. By examining how believers can maintain faith in a God who seems distant amid tragedy and unanswered prayers, we will highlight the hope that can be found in the midst of despair, inspiring a sense of optimism. Ultimately, how do we navigate the tension between trusting God's goodness and grappling with the seemingly arbitrary nature of suffering?

Facing the Abyss of Grief

Imagine a mother on her knees, pleading with God to save her child's life after a devastating car accident. She pours out her heart, begging for healing, yet despite her fervent prayers, her child slips away. In the aftermath, she grapples with the silence of God and the unbearable weight of her loss, feeling as though the very foundations of her faith have crumbled. This scenario reflects the reality for many: prayers that feel powerful in their utterance often

---

1. Lewis, *Problem of Pain*, 91.

become mere whispers against the backdrop of tragic circumstances, leaving a void where hope once resided.

The story of Mary and Martha in the Gospel of John is a poignant illustration of this experience. Their brother Lazarus lay sick, and they sent word to Jesus, confident that he would come to their aid. However, as the narrative unfolds, we see that Jesus delayed his arrival. By the time he reached Bethany, Lazarus had already been dead for four days. The sisters' anguish was palpable, each echoing the painful lament: "Lord . . . if you had been here, my brother would not have died" (John 11:21). Their sorrow mirrors our own in times of desperation, revealing a deep-seated frustration when God appears silent in our suffering. In that moment, they stood in mourning and a profound crisis of faith, questioning the very nature of God's love and presence in their darkest hour.

As they confronted their grief, the narrative captures a critical aspect of their experience: the weight of unanswered prayers. Martha, expressing her sorrow, conveyed a sentiment felt by many: the tension between faith and the reality of loss. In their desperation, Mary and Martha were not alone; they embodied the struggle of countless individuals who have faced seemingly insurmountable grief. Their cries for help, resonating with feelings of abandonment, reflect the universal human condition in the face of tragedy.

Dr. Harold G. Koenig, in his work on spirituality and health, notes that individuals often encounter crises of faith during times of intense grief, leading them to question their beliefs and the very nature of divine intervention.[2] This perspective reinforces the notion that grief does not negate faith but can deepen our understanding of it. Just as Mary and Martha grappled with their sorrow, we, too, may find ourselves wrestling with our beliefs when confronted with profound loss. The story invites us to reflect on the nature of God's timing and the mysteries of his will. Even when we feel forsaken, God is present, working in ways we cannot yet see.

---

2. Koenig, *Spirituality in Patient Care*, 153.

Abigail's Story

Abigail, the third of five siblings, was a bright, intelligent girl born into a loving Christian home. Her passion for math and science and her love for reading flourished in an environment where the family lacked luxuries like television or video games. Though her parents were farmers and often struggled to put food on the table, they always did their best to provide for Abigail and her siblings. Despite their financial hardships, their home was filled with love and care.

However, the tranquility of Abigail's idyllic childhood was abruptly shattered when she was sexually abused by an uncle and a cousin in her country of origin. In a world where she should have felt safe, her innocence was stolen, and she bore the burden of this trauma in silence, never revealing her pain to her parents. As she grappled with feelings of shame and worthlessness, she often questioned why God had allowed such suffering. "Why didn't he protect me?" she wondered, wrestling with her faith and sense of self-worth.

Abigail's life took a turn when she received a scholarship opportunity to move to the US for her college education. Despite the excitement of this new beginning, Abigail felt lost and anxious, believing that no one would ever love her due to her past.

While in college, she joined a Christian campus ministry. There, she met Jim, a sophomore who had recently attended a discipleship Bible study. Their friendship blossomed into romance, and they were baptized on the same day, marking a fresh start. Abigail felt safe with Jim; he respected her boundaries and never forced himself on her. They became the model Christian couple on campus, eventually taking on leadership roles and mentoring other couples.

As graduation approached, Jim proposed to Abigail, turning their celebration into a dual occasion—commencement and their wedding. Yet, Abigail remained unaware of how her past trauma would cast a shadow over their marriage. Soon after their honeymoon, intimacy became a challenge; every encounter triggered her PTSD, causing her to withdraw emotionally. Jim, eager to start a family, struggled to understand Abigail's struggles, and they began attending therapy together. Jim was steadfast in his support, motivated by his genuine love for her.

However, Abigail soon noticed changes in Jim. He began drinking more frequently, relying on alcohol to cope with the mounting pressure. Though he was not abusive, his behavior contradicted their Christian values, leaving Abigail feeling increasingly isolated. When she discovered his collection of pornography, her feelings of guilt and anger toward God intensified. "Why is this happening to me?" she cried out, believing that her past and her present were intertwined in ways that made her unworthy of happiness.

Determined to reconcile their relationship, Abigail and Jim agreed to try for children, believing that parenthood could help heal their wounds. After a year and a half of trying without success, they consulted a specialist who confirmed Abigail's fears: conceiving naturally would be extremely difficult. She agreed to undergo cryopreservation, a process where her eggs would be frozen and later fertilized. Jim's desire for children provided a glimmer of hope, rekindling his connection with Abigail.

When Abigail finally became pregnant, they celebrated with joy, but their happiness was short lived. At six months, she tragically lost the baby, plunging them into despair. "Where are you, Lord?" Abigail prayed, her heart aching with the weight of loss. "Why have you abandoned me when I needed you most?"

As Jim retreated further into his drinking and pornography, Abigail felt as though she was losing everything. She poured her heart out in prayer, pleading with God to allow her to have a child and save her marriage. Yet, her second pregnancy ended in heartbreak as well, shaking the very foundation of her faith.

Determined not to give up, Abigail tried once more and became pregnant with a boy. This time, she fasted and prayed fervently, asking God for a miracle. Jim, thrilled at the news, slowly began to reengage with Abigail, and hope flickered anew. The anticipation and joy that Abigail's pregnancy brought to their lives was palpable, a testament to the power of hope in the face of adversity.

When baby Jimmy was born, for a brief moment, Abigail felt that her prayers had finally been answered. The joy of holding her son in her arms brought a sense of hope she had longed for. Jim, too, seemed to come back to life—engaged, smiling, and talking about their future as a family. However, just two days later, complications arose. As Jimmy's health deteriorated, the doctors delivered the devastating news that they were unable to save him. Two weeks after his birth, their precious son passed away.

The loss shattered Abigail and Jim in different ways. Abigail, overwhelmed with grief, echoed the words of Mary and Martha: "Lord, if you had been here, my child would not have died." She felt the deep sting of abandonment by the God she had trusted so deeply.

Jim, on the other hand, became consumed by disappointment and despair. He had poured all his hope into the birth of their child, believing it would be the key to healing their marriage and restoring what had been broken between them. However, now, facing the death of their son, the weight of it all was too much. His pain caused him to withdraw further into himself. Abigail watched helplessly as Jim distanced himself emotionally and, eventually, physically.

The intimacy they had briefly rediscovered after the pregnancy vanished. Jim began spending nights away from home, drinking to numb the pain. Before long, he decided to move out of the house. The grief of losing their son had become too heavy for him to bear within the confines of their troubled marriage.

Jim's departure left Abigail devastated as she grappled not only with the loss of their child but with the unraveling of her marriage. Alone and broken, she questioned whether God had ever truly been with her, despite her years of prayers and faith.

As she navigated the depths of her sorrow, Abigail felt abandoned and betrayed by the person she had turned to for support, God. In the shadow of her loss, she found herself at a crossroads. Would she continue to seek God in her pain, or would she turn away from the faith that had sustained her through so much?

The Question of God's Absence

In the face of suffering, we often grapple with the painful question of God's presence: Why does he seem to be absent when we need him most? This inquiry resonates throughout Scripture and echoes the feelings of countless believers who have faced tragedy. The book of Psalms is replete with expressions of anguish, reflecting the deep-seated cries of the faithful who feel forsaken. For instance, Ps 22:1 states, "My God, my God, why have you forsaken me?" This lament captures the profound sense of abandonment that can accompany suffering, inviting us to confront the stark reality of our experiences.

When tragedy strikes—whether through the loss of a loved one, illness, or personal despair—it can feel as though the heavens have closed off, leaving our pleas to echo into silence. In such moments, many believers find themselves echoing the psalmist's words, longing for reassurance and a sign of divine presence. The silence of God can feel isolating, as if our cries are lost in an unresponsive void. It is within this silence that the struggle of faith becomes most pronounced. We may question our worthiness to be heard or wonder if our faith has somehow failed us.

However, it is crucial to recognize that our feelings of abandonment do not equate to God's absence. In his book *God on Mute*, Pete Greig emphasizes this point, sharing that just because God seems silent does not mean he is absent, and that sometimes God's silence is a precursor to the most extraordinary moves of God.[3] Greig's perspective serves as a powerful reminder that our emotional states do not dictate the reality of God's presence in our lives.

In John 11:35 we encounter one of the most profound truths of Scripture: "Jesus wept." This brief verse reveals the depth of Christ's compassion and empathy toward our suffering. Even in moments of silence, God is not indifferent; he enters our pain alongside us, as biblical scholar N. T. Wright notes: "Jesus's tears remind us that the God we worship is not a detached deity, but one

---

3. Greig, *God on Mute*, 105.

who understands and shares in our sorrow."[4] This understanding transforms our perception of God's absence, allowing us to recognize that even in our darkest hours, he is with us, sharing our grief and suffering.

Jesus's own experience of grief showcases the duality of his divine nature and his human experience. Throughout his earthly ministry, he faced betrayal, abandonment, and the ultimate sacrifice on the cross, expressing his anguish in words and tears. This reflection of Jesus as both fully divine and fully human gives us a glimpse into the heart of God: a God who is intimately familiar with our suffering. It reassures us that our grief is valid and acknowledged by the Creator of the universe, who knows the depths of our pain because he has experienced it himself.

Furthermore, the silence we experience can be viewed as a profound invitation to deepen our faith. In those moments when we feel that God is distant, we are challenged to cultivate a relationship built on trust rather than solely on the need for answers. This transformation requires a shift in perspective—recognizing that God's ways are not our ways, and his timing often transcends our understanding. The silence of God can serve as a space for growth, where our faith is tested and strengthened. As Wright explains, "Faith is the confidence that God is present and active, even when we do not perceive it."[5] This assertion encourages us to seek God not only in our victories but also in our struggles, fostering a faith that is resilient in the face of adversity.

Ultimately, the question of God's absence invites us to explore the complexities of faith and the mystery of divine timing. While we may not always understand why God appears silent, we are called to hold on to the promise of his presence. In our suffering, we can find solace in the knowledge that God is intimately aware of our pain, transforming our moments of despair into opportunities for deeper trust and reliance on his goodness. In Isa 41:10 God reassures us: "So do not fear, for I am with you; do not be dismayed, for I am your God." This promise can be a lifeline for

---

4. Wright, *Simply Jesus*, 150.
5. Wright, *Simply Jesus*, 152.

those navigating the depths of grief and sorrow, reminding us that we are never truly alone.

The exploration of God's apparent absence in times of suffering serves as a poignant reminder of the complexities of faith. Our feelings of abandonment, while profoundly real, do not define our relationship with God. Instead, they can lead us to a deeper understanding of his love and presence in our lives, even amid pain. By embracing the reality of our grief and trusting in God's enduring compassion, we can navigate our journeys of sorrow with hope and resilience.

The Unanswered Call: The Story of Lazarus

The story of Lazarus profoundly reflects the tension between faith and silence. Lazarus, a dear friend of Jesus, became gravely ill, prompting his sisters, Mary and Martha, to send an urgent message: "Lord, the one you love is sick" (John 11:3). This message was more than just a report of Lazarus's condition—it was a heartfelt plea for help, a prayer born from deep faith and trust. The phrase "the one you love" reveals the depth of the relationship between Jesus and Lazarus. Their bond was personal, marked by mutual care and affection. Lazarus was not just another follower; he was someone Jesus truly loved, a close companion. Mary and Martha had no doubt that Jesus had the power to save their brother—they had witnessed his miraculous healings, his authority over demons, and even his ability to raise the dead. Their faith in him was unwavering.

However, instead of rushing to Lazarus's side, Jesus did something unexpected—he delayed. He stayed where he was for two days, attending to other matters while Lazarus's condition worsened. This delay is perhaps one of the most perplexing aspects of the story. Why would Jesus, known for his compassion and love, not respond immediately to this desperate cry for help? Why, when he had the power to intervene and prevent the inevitable, would he allow Lazarus to die?

For Mary and Martha, this delay must have felt like a painful silence from God. Their heartfelt plea was met with inaction, and the worst possible outcome unfolded—Lazarus died. Their grief, compounded by confusion, gave way to heart-wrenching questions. They believed that Jesus would come in time, yet he didn't. Where was he when they needed him most? Had he abandoned them in their darkest moment? Their pain is relatable to anyone who has ever prayed fervently for something only to face silence in return.

Even Jesus's disciples, who had witnessed countless miracles and shared in his ministry, were puzzled by his decision to delay. They, too, loved Lazarus and understood how much he meant to Jesus. They questioned his judgment when they saw him staying away while Lazarus was critically ill. Why wasn't he rushing to save his beloved friend? What could possibly be more important than responding to such an urgent need?

When the disciples voiced their concerns, Jesus responded with words that seemed cryptic and even detached: "This sickness will not end in death. No, it is for God's glory so that God's Son may be glorified through it" (John 11:4). To those hearing these words for the first time, they might have seemed cold or confusing. How could an illness that led to death be part of God's plan for glory? How could allowing such profound pain and suffering serve a higher purpose?

In the eyes of those around him, Jesus's delay may have seemed like a grave mistake or a lack of care. However, they could not see at that moment that this delay was part of a much larger purpose. Jesus knew that Lazarus would die, but he also knew that death wouldn't have the final word. His delay was not a sign of neglect but a deliberate choice to reveal something greater than just healing—it was to reveal the power of resurrection.

When Jesus finally arrived in Bethany, Martha ran to meet him with the words, "Lord . . . if you had been here, my brother would not have died" (John 11:21). Later, Mary echoed the same sentiment (John 11:32). Both sisters expressed a mixture of faith and frustration—a belief that Jesus could have prevented the

THE SILENCE OF GOD IN OUR SUFFERING

tragedy, and yet a sense of confusion over why he didn't. It's a feeling that many believers can relate to when prayers seem to go unanswered, and God seems distant in times of deep loss.

But Jesus, in his divine wisdom, was operating according to a different timeline. In the midst of their grief, he wept with them, showing that he deeply understood their pain (John 11:35). His tears revealed that he was not indifferent to their suffering; he was fully present in their sorrow. And then, in a moment that defied all expectations, Jesus called Lazarus out of the tomb, raising him from the dead (John 11:43-44). The very event that had caused the greatest despair became the moment through which God's glory was most clearly revealed.

This story highlights a critical aspect of faith: God's timing and purposes often defy human expectations. In moments when it seems like God is silent, he may be orchestrating events in ways we cannot immediately understand. The delay was not about indifference or a lack of love but about revealing a deeper truth—God's sovereignty over life and death itself. What seemed like an unanswered prayer turned into one of the most profound demonstrations of Jesus's divine power.

For those walking through seasons of silence, the story of Lazarus offers a powerful invitation to reflect on the nature of God's response to suffering. It teaches that even when we feel abandoned or our prayers seem to go unanswered, God may be preparing a revelation of his glory greater than we could imagine. While the waiting can be painful and the silence deafening, this story reminds us that Jesus is never truly absent. He hears, he cares, and he acts—though often in ways that transcend our immediate understanding.

Ultimately, the story of Lazarus points to the heart of the Christian faith: the hope of resurrection, the promise that death and suffering do not have the final word. Just as Jesus brought Lazarus out of the grave, he offers hope that transcends our darkest moments of silence and grief. Even when the answer seems delayed, God is still at work, preparing to bring life out of death and joy out of sorrow.

A Sibling's Cry for Help: The Story of Sonia and Carlos

My mother's name is Sonia, and she is the fourth of five siblings born to my grandparents, Gilberto and Sinda. She was born in Ponce, Puerto Rico, right in the center of town. When she was just six years old, my grandparents moved to a community called El Tuque, in the mountains on the west side of Ponce, where they, like many other families, squatted on land. My grandparents were modest but provided everything my mother and her siblings needed. Like most of the island, they were Catholic, though they did not have strong Christian values or deep biblical knowledge.

Of all her siblings, my mother was closest to her brother Carlos, the middle child. They were inseparable and did everything together, their bond strengthened by being only fifteen months apart. As the only boy, Carlos was treated like the prince of the house—or, as my mom would say, he was "el nene de la casa" (the baby of the house). At times, my mother often felt overshadowed by the attention Carlos received, but their relationship remained strong.

Carlos was the constant in my mother's life; later, he became a similar figure for me. After my parents separated, my father moved to Chicago and Carlos became the male figure I looked up to. He was not just my uncle, he was like a father to me. Despite his flaws and struggles, Carlos was the one I watched closely, even though the path he walked was not one anyone would wish for.

Carlos and Sonia were the life of every party and family gathering. They danced, laughed, and were excellent jokers. A party was not a party if they were not there. When I was about ten years old, during one of the parties at our house, I snuck a beer, wanting to impress my friends. Carlos caught me, opened the beer, and handed it to me, saying, "You want to drink? Go ahead." I hesitated, but he was firm. "I'm not asking. I'm telling you." When I finally took a sip and grimaced, he looked me in the eye and said, "It's disgusting, isn't it? Why would you want something so awful?"

Then, in a moment I'll never forget, he said, "Do not be like me, Mel. You are meant for great things, and this won't take you there."

Carlos's words were like a prophecy over my life, spoken by the very man I admired most. But as I grew older, I watched Carlos sink deeper into addiction. Alcohol turned into harder substances, and though he still cared for our family, the drugs took the best of him. Despite his struggles, Carlos remained close to my mother, and their bond never wavered. He was still her protector, her confidant, and for me, the only present father figure I had during those years. Our family bond, though tested, remained unbreakable.

In 1998, after years of battling drugs and alcohol, Carlos contracted pneumonia and was hospitalized. It became clear that his body was giving up. As always, my grandmother and mother were by his side. Desperate to save her brother, my mom prayed fervently and made a promise to God—that if he healed Carlos, she would dedicate her life to God.

But Carlos's condition worsened. The drugs had ravaged his body, and he was now battling severe withdrawals. In his desperation, he begged my mom to find heroin to ease his pain. Torn between her love for her brother and her fear of doing the wrong thing, she refused, choosing instead to trust in God's healing. But that healing never came. Carlos passed away in the hospital, his breath taken by the very addictions that had gripped him for so long.

My mom was shattered. She blamed herself for his death, wondering if her decision not to get him the drugs had hastened his end. She also blamed God. Why hadn't he answered her prayers? After almost losing my brother Freddy, now her brother—her best friend, her protector—was gone.

The weight of Carlos's death changed everything. My mom, once the life of every party, slipped into a deep depression. The music stopped. The dancing ended. The joy that had once filled our home was replaced by an emptiness we could all feel. Carlos, my uncle, my father figure, was gone. However, his words to me—"You're meant for great things"—stayed with me. They echoed with a promise I would later realize only God could fulfill.

When crisis hits, we can always choose to see God through our tears, finding his presence in our pain. Or, like Sonia, we can shut ourselves off and allow sorrow to consume us. The choice is ours, and it's one that defines how we move forward—whether we let our grief draw us closer to God or push us further away.

Why the Silence?

Why did Jesus allow Mary and Martha to endure such anguish before acting? This question lingers for many of us who have faced unanswered prayers. Why does God permit us to experience pain and suffering when he has the power to intervene? The story of Lazarus invites us to confront these difficult questions head-on, revealing profound truths about faith, timing, and the nature of divine love.

The silence of God in our suffering can often feel like abandonment. However, the narrative of Lazarus reveals that God's silence is not a sign of his absence; instead, it highlights the complexity of his plans, which often extend beyond our immediate understanding. In this case, Jesus's delay was not indifference but part of a larger plan to reveal the glory of God profoundly. As theologian N. T. Wright suggests, "God is not simply a spectator of our suffering, but a participant in it."[6] This understanding reshapes our perception of silence; it is not an absence of action but a space in which God prepares us for something greater.

When Jesus finally arrived in Bethany, he did so with a purpose that transcended mere healing. His delay allowed him to demonstrate his authority over death itself. Ultimately, when he called Lazarus out of the tomb, it was not just a miracle of resurrection; it was a declaration of his divine power and a foretaste of his ultimate victory over the grave. Jesus declared, "I am the resurrection and the life" (John 11:25), affirming that those who believe in him will never truly die. This moment serves as a testament to

---

6. Wright, *Simply Jesus*, 89.

the hope that sustains us amid grief and loss, reassuring us of his ultimate victory and comforting us in our times of need.

Yet, even in the glory of Lazarus's resurrection, the pain of loss still mattered. Jesus did not rush past the grief; he entered into it. In doing so, he acknowledged that suffering is a part of the human experience that cannot be overlooked or minimized. This tells us that while God may not always answer our prayers as we expect, he is never detached from our suffering. His silence does not imply neglect; instead, it invites deeper faith and trust in his perfect timing.

As we grapple with unanswered prayers and the silence of God, we can find comfort in the fact that he weeps with us and stands with us in our darkest moments, even when his purposes remain hidden. The God who allowed Lazarus to die is also the God who raised him from the dead, reminding us that the story does not end in despair. Rather, it leads us toward hope and transformation, encouraging us to trust in the one who holds our pain and our future in his hands and filling us with hope and encouragement for the journey ahead.

A God Who Weeps with Us

When Jesus finally made his way to Bethany, the emotional weight of the situation was overwhelming. Lazarus had been in the tomb for four days, and the grief in the community was palpable. Martha and Mary, broken by their brother's death, greeted Jesus with the exact heart-wrenching words: "Lord, if you had been here, my brother would not have died" (John 11:21, 32). These words are familiar to anyone who has ever cried out in desperation during moments of loss, wondering why God did not intervene. They echo the questions so many of us have when faced with tragedy: Why did God allow this? Where was he?

In response to their pain, we see something remarkable. The Gospel tells us that Jesus was "deeply moved in spirit and troubled" (John 11:33). This reaction was not mere sympathy or a casual acknowledgment of their sorrow. The Greek words used here suggest a profound emotional response—a deep disturbance within his spirit that transcended ordinary compassion. Jesus was not only sharing in the grief of Martha, Mary, and the mourners; he was also profoundly affected by the reality of death and the suffering it brought into the world. His spirit was troubled not just by the loss of his friend Lazarus but by the broader implications of sin and mortality that led to such sorrow. In this moment, Jesus revealed his empathetic nature, reminding us that he is not distant from our pain but instead intimately connected to it, sharing in our heartache as he confronts the brokenness of humanity.

Then, in one of the shortest yet most powerful verses in Scripture, "Jesus wept" (John 11:35). Despite knowing he was about to raise Lazarus from the dead, Jesus did not rush past the moment's sorrow. Instead, he allowed himself to be fully present in it. His tears were not for show; they revealed a God who does not stand apart from human suffering but fully enters into it. Craig Keener notes that Jesus's weeping demonstrates his empathy, showing that he is deeply affected by the pain of others, even when he knows a miracle is forthcoming.[7]

This simple verse, "Jesus wept," offers a profound revelation about the heart of God. Although he possesses all power and authority, he does not remain distant from the pain of his people. Jesus could have prevented Lazarus's death altogether. However, he chose to allow this moment of grief, not because he was indifferent, but because he wanted to reveal something greater about his character. Darrell Bock emphasizes that Jesus's emotional engagement with grief is essential to understanding his mission and the nature of God's love.[8] The fact that he wept even when he knew the end of the story—that Lazarus would soon walk out of the tomb—shows that our pain is not minimized in God's eyes. It is not rushed through or dismissed. God does not demand that we move quickly past our grief; instead, he meets us in it.

This scene illustrates the mystery of God's timing. Jesus had the power to heal Lazarus before he died, yet he allowed his friend

---

7. Keener, *Gospel of John*, 2:245–46.
8. Bock with Simpson, *Jesus According to Scripture*, 573.

to pass away. For many, this delay might seem like a failure or a lack of care. However, Jesus's actions challenge us to rethink what it means when God does not answer our prayers in the way we expect or when we want him to. His delay was not neglect; it was purposeful. By waiting, Jesus not only set the stage for a greater miracle but also demonstrated that he is not just the God of solutions but the God who enters into our suffering before bringing restoration.

Jesus's tears also teach us that grief is not a lack of faith. Too often, we feel the need to suppress our emotions during difficult times, thinking that showing sadness or despair might indicate weak faith. However, Jesus, the embodiment of faith, wept. He did not rush to display his power; instead, he paused and embraced the moment's sorrow. His tears permit us to grieve, to express our pain, and to do so without feeling that we are somehow letting God down.

Moreover, Jesus's weeping points to the fact that suffering, while deeply painful, is a place where we can uniquely encounter God's presence. Psalm 56:8 reminds us that God keeps track of all our sorrows, collecting our tears in a bottle. This image conveys the idea that God never overlooks or forgets our pain. When Jesus wept, he showed us that our tears matter to him. Our suffering is not ignored; it is shared by the very one who holds all things together.

The depth of Jesus's empathy is one of the most compelling aspects of his character. As Heb 4:15 tells us, "For we do not have a high priest who is unable to empathize with our weaknesses, but we have one who has been tempted in every way, just as we are—yet he did not sin." Jesus understands the full range of human experience, including the depths of our pain. This means that when we suffer, we are not alone. Jesus is right there with us, weeping alongside us, and offering his presence as comfort.

In many ways, this moment in Bethany challenges our understanding of God. If Jesus, knowing the outcome, chose to weep, then surely our tears in the face of tragedy are not a sign of weak faith but of trust. They signify that we believe God is with us in the valley of the shadow of death. They recognize that while we do not always understand his ways, we trust he is near to the brokenhearted (Ps 34:18).

The scene at Lazarus's tomb also invites us to reconsider the purpose of our suffering. So often, we want to move past pain as quickly as possible, eager for the resolution and the joy that comes afterward. However, Jesus teaches us that God's presence in our suffering is as significant as the miracle that may come later. In the middle of our tears, we encounter a God who is not indifferent but deeply moved by our pain. We find a God who weeps with us and, in doing so, offers us the profound comfort of his love.

As we reflect on this passage, we are reminded that we have a choice in every moment of grief and loss. Like Martha and Mary, we can bring our pain to Jesus, trusting that he understands and shares in it. Alternatively, we can close ourselves off, letting our sorrow consume us. However, if we choose to bring our tears to the feet of the Savior, we will find a God who weeps with us and who, in time, will bring the restoration we so deeply long for.

The Hard Reality of Unanswered Prayers

For many, the end of the story is not a resurrection but a lingering grief. A marriage still ends; a loved one still passes away; a tragedy unfolds despite desperate prayers. The heart-wrenching question emerges: What do we do when God's silence seems permanent? The story of Lazarus serves as a poignant reminder that even when we do not understand why we experience suffering, we can trust that God is present in our pain. He may not prevent every hardship, but he promises to walk through it with us, sharing our sorrows and offering comfort amid despair.

This chapter challenges us to wrestle with these difficult truths, just as Mary and Martha did. Their grief and disappointment were palpable, mirroring the emotions many of us carry in our hearts. The weight of loss can feel suffocating, and yet, amid their despair, they encountered Jesus—a Savior who holds the power of life and death and intimately shares in our deepest

THE SILENCE OF GOD IN OUR SUFFERING

sorrows. This powerful interaction illustrates that God does not distance himself from our pain; instead, he enters into it, showing us that our grief is not in vain.[9]

As I reflect on my own experiences of unanswered prayers and the moments when I felt God's silence enveloping me, I am reminded of Mary and Martha. They sent their message in faith, trusting that Jesus would come to their aid. When he didn't arrive as expected, they bore the full weight of loss and confusion, grappling with the reality of their unmet expectations. However, in the end, they experienced the depth of his love and compassion in ways they could not have imagined. Jesus did not simply restore Lazarus to life; he revealed a deeper truth about his nature and the hope that comes from trusting in him, even amid profound grief.[10]

This story invites us to embrace our struggles and wrestle with our doubts, knowing that our unanswered prayers do not diminish our faith. Instead, they can lead us into a deeper relationship with a God who understands our pain, hears our cries, and promises never to leave us alone. We are not alone in our waiting or our grief; our struggles can serve as a bridge to a more profound encounter with God's presence, allowing us to witness his faithfulness even when we cannot see the path ahead. Ultimately, in our darkest moments, the light of God's love shines the brightest, guiding us toward healing and hope.[11]

Conclusion: Embracing the Mystery of Faith

As we conclude this chapter, we acknowledge that faith does not always provide neat answers or resolutions. Instead, it invites us to lean into the mystery of God's presence in our suffering. While we may never fully comprehend why some prayers go unanswered, we can find hope in the promise that God is with us in our pain.

---

9. Keener, *Gospel of John*, 2:245–46.
10. Bock with Simpson, *Jesus According to Scripture*, 573.
11. Wright, *Simply Jesus*, 89.

The silence of God can be a source of deep frustration, yet it can also lead us to a profound encounter with his grace. As we learn to navigate the complexities of faith and suffering, may we find solace in knowing that we are never truly alone. In our darkest moments, God weeps with us, inviting us to bring our pain to him, and offering a love that transcends our understanding.

Application

Take a moment to reflect on how you have responded to the silence of God in your life. Have feelings of abandonment, frustration, or despair ever overshadowed your faith? It is easy, amid personal crises and unanswered prayers, to feel isolated and question God's presence. However, the story of Lazarus teaches us a different perspective. In times of loss, how can you begin to recognize God's presence amid the silence? Reflecting on your past responses can guide you toward a more faith-filled approach in future challenges.

Consider the role of prayer during these difficult times. Have you expressed your honest feelings to God, including your doubts and questions, or have you hesitated, fearing that your cries might go unheard? Challenge yourself to embrace an authentic prayer life—one that encompasses your pain and uncertainty while trusting in God's love and understanding. Remember that even when it feels as though your prayers go unanswered, God walks with you in your suffering. He is present in your grief and is working in ways that may not be immediately apparent.

As you move forward, remember that God invites you to lay your burdens at his feet. He desires to meet you in your pain, walk alongside you in your darkest moments, and bring healing, even when it is not in the form you expect.

Reflection Questions

1. How have you felt God's presence during times of silence or unanswered prayers?
2. In what ways can you foster a more authentic dialogue with God in your prayer life?
3. Reflect on a time when you experienced a sense of God's nearness amid your suffering. What did that reveal about his character?
4. How can you support others who are struggling with unanswered prayers and feelings of abandonment?

Closing Prayer

Lord, we come to you with our heartaches and questions, just as Mary and Martha did. When we feel overwhelmed by grief and silence, help us to remember that you are near, ready to hear and comfort us in our pain. Teach us to bring our honest prayers before you, trusting in your compassion and understanding. Guide us through our moments of despair, and may we find strength in your presence, even when we feel abandoned. Transform our hurt into hope, our doubt into faith, and our isolation into communion with you. Let your will be done in our lives as we rest in the assurance that you are always with us, even in our darkest hours. In Jesus's name, we pray. Amen.

CHAPTER 6

Why Do Bad Things Happen to Good People?

The Lord is righteous in all his ways and faithful in all he does.
—Psalm 145:17

Introduction

In life, we all encounter moments when tragedy strikes without warning, disrupting our sense of stability and leaving us searching for answers. Sometimes, it happens to those we least expect—good people who are kind, faithful, loving, and dedicated to serving others. These individuals seem to embody everything we aspire to be, yet they, too, are not immune to the pain and suffering that life can bring.

For centuries, theologians, philosophers, and believers have wrestled with the perplexing question: If God is good and all powerful, why does he allow bad things to happen to good people? This question cuts deep, stirring intellectual curiosity and emotional turmoil as we are forced to confront the harsh realities of life that do not seem to align with our understanding of God's character. Why would a loving God permit such suffering, and how can we reconcile his goodness with the apparent randomness and unfairness of tragedy?

These questions are not easily answered, and the Bible does not provide a simple, one-size-fits-all explanation for the problem of suffering. Instead, it offers stories, wisdom, and truths that help guide us through these painful moments, offering a perspective deeply rooted in faith. This chapter seeks to explore these difficult and timeless questions while offering a biblically grounded perspective on the issue of suffering. It draws upon Scripture, personal experience, and the experiences of others to provide hope and insight, even when clear answers remain elusive. Our faith, we believe, is a source of reassurance and strength, even in the face of life's most challenging moments.

A Personal Experience

The reality of these questions is unfolding for me right now. As I sit in the hospital, watching these events take place, I am writing this chapter in real time, grappling with the weight of what is happening before my eyes.

It all began on Wednesday, October 16, 2024, a day that started like any other. After picking up my son from school, I prepared for our usual Wednesday-night routine at church. Our evenings are typically reserved for youth group, Spanish group, and prayer, so we rarely make other plans. However, that day was different. My wife, Jeanette, sent me a message with a special request: she had been given courtside tickets to the Chicago Bulls vs. Minnesota Timberwolves game. She asked if I could excuse myself from church for the evening to go on a date with her.

Having never been to a Bulls game at the United Center, let alone courtside, I decided to make an exception. It felt like a once-in-a-lifetime opportunity, so I agreed and headed out. As the second quarter was about to start, my phone rang. It was my cousin Abraham—unusual for that time of night. Normally, I would not answer when I'm out with Jeanette, but something told me I needed to pick up. The moment I answered, I could hear the fear and tremble in his voice.

"They found Denise unresponsive," he said. Denise, his spouse, had been rushed to the hospital, and the doctors found bleeding in her brain—a possible hemorrhage. After being taken to a local emergency room, she was airlifted to Lutheran General Hospital in Park Ridge, Illinois. I immediately offered to come, but Abraham asked me to wait an hour until they completed her transport and had more information.

We stayed until we received the call from Abraham, who was arriving at the hospital and asked us to join him. When we arrived, I saw Abraham, his two youngest sons, ages seven and eight, and Denise's sisters and father gathered in a consultation room. They were on the phone with the doctor, who delivered the heartbreaking news. Denise had been suffering from headaches for about a month. Although Abraham had urged her to get checked, she had dismissed it, thinking it was early menopause, and had been taking over-the-counter medication. What they didn't know was that she had been developing a hemorrhage. By the time it was discovered, it was too late—Denise was not showing any signs of brain activity.

We were all in shock. Denise was one of the kindest, most caring people I knew. She was a faithful volunteer in our children's ministry, part of the welcome team, and loved by everyone at the church. She was a devoted wife and mother with a heart of gold, always willing to help and always full of grace. It was impossible to believe that something like this could happen to her.

As I stood there, hearing the doctor's words and watching the family crumble in pain, I found myself at a loss for words. Despite all my pastoral experience and training, I could not find the right words to say. I have a doctorate in preaching—I should have known what to say—but at that moment, there were no words. All I could do was cry with them, hold them, and be present in their grief.

Shattered by the news, Denise's boys kept asking the same question that was on all our hearts: "Why her? Why did she have to die?" I had no answers that could ease their pain, no explanation that could touch the depth of their grief, their loss, their new reality.

WHY DO BAD THINGS HAPPEN TO GOOD PEOPLE?

More family members arrived the following day, including Denise's oldest son, Anthony, and her mother, who had been visiting family in Mexico. There was still a flicker of hope in the room as we gathered to pray over her, asking God for a miracle, for her to wake up. However, around 2:30 p.m., the doctors met with the immediate family once again to confirm what we feared most: Denise was brain dead. Only the machines were keeping her alive. The doctors explained that they would perform one final test to check for any signs of brain activity.

At 4:37 p.m. on Thursday, October 17, 2024, they pronounced her time of death. Jeanette and I prayed with Abraham and the children—Anthony, Edgar (Abraham's son), Cristiano (8), and Zekie (7). I also prayed with Denise's parents and her sisters. Afterward, we walked to the room where Denise lay, still connected to the machines. As an organ donor, she would soon be taken for the process of collecting her organs. They gave the family time to say their final goodbyes, cry, and pray.

When everyone had their moment, Denise was taken away. A beautiful, young, promising life had come to an end.

But why her? Why would this happen to such a good person, a woman who loved God and brought joy to so many? Why do bad things happen to good people? We all face these questions, and sometimes, there are no answers—only faith and the comfort of God's presence in the midst of our deepest pain.

The Reality of a Broken World

The Bible tells us that we live in a fallen world, one that has been marred by sin ever since Adam and Eve disobeyed God in the garden of Eden (Rom 5:12). This act of disobedience is referred to in Christian theology as original sin, and it ushered in death, decay, and suffering, which have since become part of the human experience. Augustine, in *The City of God*, explains how this initial rebellion fractured the harmonious relationship between humanity and

God. As a result, suffering and death permeate creation.[1] No matter how righteous we strive to be, we cannot escape the reality of a broken world. Illness, loss, and tragedies, like the untimely passing of Denise, are all manifestations of this brokenness.

Suffering, as seen through Scripture, is a universal experience. It is not reserved for those who do wrong, but is part of the human condition in a world stained by sin. In John 16:33 Jesus himself acknowledges this when he says, "In this world you will have trouble. But take heart! I have overcome the world." These words offer profound hope amid suffering. Jesus's recognition of the inevitability of hardship does not indicate God's absence; instead, it is a reminder that suffering is part of life in this fallen world. However, even in this reality, Christ's assurance provides hope—he has triumphed over the brokenness of the world.

When tragedies occur, such as the loss of Denise, it is natural to question why God allows such pain. It can even feel as though God has overlooked or abandoned us. However, suffering is not evidence of God's absence. Rather, it points to the effects of living in an imperfect world where sin and human frailty reign. The apostle Paul writes in Rom 8:22, "We know that the whole creation has been groaning as in the pains of childbirth right up to the present time." This imagery of groaning creation speaks to the profound depth of suffering that characterizes our world. Yet, as theologian Jürgen Moltmann observes, God does not stand distant from our suffering. In *The Crucified God*, Moltmann argues that through the cross, God not only witnesses but shares in human suffering.[2] Christ's crucifixion becomes the ultimate expression of divine solidarity with a suffering world.

This brokenness and suffering, however, do not negate the goodness of God. On the contrary, they highlight humanity's need for a Savior. The suffering we experience, including the death of loved ones, reminds us that the world is not as it should be. The assurance in John 16:33 that Christ has overcome the world speaks of the ultimate victory over sin and death through Jesus's death

---

1. Augustine, *City of God* 22.22.
2. Moltmann, *Crucified God*, 47.

and resurrection. His triumph over death provides hope that while we may experience pain in this life, we are not without hope. One day, as promised in Rev 21:4, "He will wipe every tear from their eyes. There will be no more death or mourning or crying or pain, for the old order of things has passed away."

The question of why suffering exists has occupied theologians for centuries. In reflecting on the presence of evil in a world created by a good God, Augustine concludes that suffering ultimately results from humanity's misuse of free will. In his wisdom, God allows suffering as part of his divine plan to bring about a greater good. This, however, does not mean that God is the author of evil. Instead, he redeems suffering to deepen faith and lead individuals closer to him.[3] While this does not always provide immediate comfort, it invites us to trust in God's greater plan, even when we do not fully understand it.

In this sense, suffering does not exist apart from the reality of God's love and redemption. Leon Morris points out that in the Gospel of John, Jesus's suffering is not an accident or a failure but is intricately connected to God's redemptive purpose.[4] The cross becomes the symbol of both suffering and victory. Through it, Christ defeats death, not by avoiding it but by enduring and overcoming it.

As tragic as it is, the reality of a broken world also points us to the hope of redemption. This hope does not deny the pain we experience. However, it places it within the larger narrative of God's ultimate plan to restore creation. While we live in a world marred by sin, we are invited to trust in the promise that God is making all things new (Rev 21:5). Through Christ, there is hope beyond brokenness. As Jürgen Moltmann suggests, God's participation in human suffering through Christ means that he is not indifferent but is actively working to bring healing and restoration to all creation. Our hope lies in God's promise that, despite the pain and

---

3. Augustine, *City of God* 22.22.
4. Morris, *Gospel According to John*, 549.

sorrow we face, he has already secured victory over death, and one day, all suffering will end.[5]

In moments of profound loss, like Denise's passing, we are reminded that we live in a fallen world. Yet, amid this brokenness, the Bible offers a message of hope. Through Christ's victory on the cross, suffering is not the final word. One day, all things will be made new, and we will experience the fullness of life in God's redeemed creation.

God's Sovereignty and Our Limited Perspective

One of the most challenging aspects of suffering is grappling with understanding God's purposes amid pain and hardship. The reality is that human perspective is inherently limited. We often find ourselves caught in the throes of our circumstances, searching for clarity and answers that may remain elusive. In moments of anguish, it can be difficult to comprehend the broader narrative that God is weaving through our lives. This struggle is beautifully encapsulated in Isa 55:8–9, which states, "For my thoughts are not your thoughts, neither are your ways my ways." This passage serves as a humbling reminder that God's wisdom far exceeds our understanding, and his plans often operate on a divine timeline that we cannot fully grasp.

There are instances in our lives where the weight of suffering can feel unbearable, and the reasons behind our trials seem incomprehensible. In these moments, it is natural to question God's intentions and wonder why we must endure such pain. However, even when we cannot see or understand the reasons for our suffering, we can hold fast to the truth of God's sovereignty. Romans 8:28 reassures us: "And we know that in all things God works for the good of those who love him, who have been called according to his purpose." This verse serves as a cornerstone of hope, reminding us that God's overarching plan is always aimed at our ultimate good, even when circumstances seem to contradict this truth.

---

5. Moltmann, *Crucified God*, 47.

Consider the story of Joseph, who experienced profound suffering yet ultimately witnessed God's sovereign hand at work in his life. Sold into slavery by his brothers and wrongfully imprisoned, Joseph faced betrayal and hardship that tested his faith and resilience. Yet, throughout his trials, Joseph remained steadfast, trusting in God's greater plan. In Gen 50:20 he reassures his brothers, saying, "You intended to harm me, but God intended it for good to accomplish what is now being done, the saving of many lives." Here, Joseph recognizes that what was intended for evil was ultimately used by God for good—a powerful testimony to the sovereignty of God amid human suffering.

While our perspective may be limited, God's viewpoint encompasses the entirety of existence. He sees the beginning and the end, the intricate tapestry of life woven with threads of joy and sorrow. When we experience suffering, it is often difficult to discern the lessons or growth that may emerge from our pain. Yet, God invites us to trust him, even when the path ahead appears obscured. This act of faith is not just a leap into the unknown; it is a powerful connection to God's promise that he is in control, empowering us to navigate our suffering with his guidance.

It is also essential to acknowledge that suffering is not always the result of our choices or actions. Sometimes, it is a consequence of living in a broken world marred by sin and imperfection. Yet, even in these moments, we can trust that God's sovereignty remains unchanged. He is not distant or indifferent to our suffering but intimately acquainted with our pain. Jesus himself experienced deep anguish and sorrow during his time on earth, ultimately culminating in his crucifixion. Through his suffering, he demonstrated God's profound love and solidarity with humanity, showing that our pain does not go unnoticed.

In times of hardship, we can find comfort in knowing that we are not alone in our struggles. God walks alongside us, his presence offering strength and guidance as we navigate our suffering. While we may not understand the "why" behind our circumstances, we can find comfort in the certainty of God's goodness and faithfulness. Our trust in him becomes a powerful testament to our faith, even in the face of uncertainty.

Ultimately, our limited perspective can be a source of growth, teaching us to rely more deeply on God's promises and character. As we confront life's challenges, we are invited to embrace the mystery of faith, knowing that God is sovereign, and his plans will unfold in ways that bring about our ultimate good. By acknowledging our limitations and placing our trust in God's greater understanding, we can find hope and peace amid our trials, confident that he is working all things together for our benefit.

In light of this theme, theologian R. C. Sproul emphasizes the necessity of trusting in God's sovereignty, writing, "There are no maverick molecules running around loose. God is sovereign. God is God."[6] This powerful assertion encourages believers to maintain faith in God's providence, even when faced with the mystery of suffering.

The Role of Free Will

Another significant aspect to consider when grappling with the question of suffering is the role of free will. God created humanity with the inherent ability to choose, granting us the freedom to make decisions that can lead to suffering, both for ourselves and for others. This gift of free will is foundational to what it means to be human, as it allows for genuine love, relationships, and moral responsibility. However, it also means that our choices can have profound consequences, leading to pain and suffering in a world where sin exists.

C. S. Lewis poignantly addresses this in his book *The Problem of Pain*, stating, "God created things that had free will. That means creatures that can go wrong if they choose."[7] He further explains that much of the evil and suffering present in the world can be attributed to human choices, illustrating that the capacity to choose

---

6. Sproul, *Chosen by God*, 27.
7. Lewis, *Problem of Pain*, 40.

is both a gift and a burden. While this perspective may not fully answer the question of why good people suffer, it serves as a vital reminder that free will is essential for genuine love and a meaningful relationship with God.

The presence of free will also highlights the complexity of human relationships and the reality that our actions can impact others. For instance, when individuals make selfish or harmful choices, those decisions can inflict pain on innocent people. This interconnectedness underscores the tragic reality that suffering is not always a direct result of one's personal actions but can stem from the collective choices of humanity. In a world where free will exists, the potential for both good and evil is woven into the fabric of human experience.

Moreover, the exercise of free will brings with it the possibility of choosing to love, serve, and honor God. Genuine love cannot be coerced; it must be freely given. In this sense, suffering can sometimes be a consequence of living in a world where love and choice coexist. The freedom to choose means that we are also free to make choices that can lead to suffering for ourselves or others. This dynamic invites us to engage in self-reflection and accountability as we navigate our lives.

Ultimately, the concept of free will reminds us that God values our choices and desires a relationship with us based on love and trust. Although we may struggle to comprehend the full implications of suffering, we can find comfort in the knowledge that God's gift of free will is integral to our humanity. Even in the face of suffering, we are invited to exercise our free will in ways that reflect God's love, grace, and redemptive purposes.

In understanding free will, it is essential to recognize that it comes with the capacity for moral growth and the opportunity for redemption. The struggles and challenges we face in life can lead us to a deeper understanding of ourselves and our relationship with God. When we make poor choices, we are not beyond redemption; rather, we are given the chance to learn from our mistakes and grow in our faith. This notion aligns with the idea that suffering can serve as a catalyst for transformation, prompting individuals to seek healing, forgiveness, and a closer walk with God. As the apostle Paul writes in Rom 5:3–4, "Not only so, but we also glory in our sufferings, because we know that suffering produces perseverance; perseverance, character; and character, hope." This passage highlights how our struggles can ultimately lead us toward spiritual maturity and a more profound reliance on God's grace.

Furthermore, acknowledging the role of free will compels us to respond to the suffering of others with empathy and compassion. Understanding that everyone is navigating their own choices and challenges can inspire us to be agents of love and support in a broken world. When we witness someone else's suffering, we are reminded of the interconnectedness of humanity and the responsibility we have to uplift one another. This perspective invites us to extend grace, offer help, and create a community where love prevails over suffering. By actively choosing to embody God's love, we contribute to healing a world that often seems consumed by pain. In this way, the exercise of free will becomes a personal journey and a collective endeavor to reflect God's character and purposes in a world desperately in need of hope.

Suffering and Redemption

Though we may not always understand why we suffer, the Christian faith offers the hope of redemption. Jesus Christ, who was without sin, suffered the ultimate injustice when he was crucified on the cross. His suffering, however, was not in vain. He offered salvation and the hope of eternal life through his death and resurrection. As Burton Z. Cooper notes, "The cross is the ultimate sign that God does not abandon us in our suffering but enters into it with us."[8] This profound truth emphasizes that God is not distant from our pain; instead, he actively participates in our suffering, providing comfort and assurance that we are not alone. This divine companionship comforts us in our moments of despair. It transforms our

---

8. Cooper, *Why God?*, 89.

understanding of suffering from a purely negative experience into an opportunity for profound spiritual growth.

The suffering of Christ serves as a powerful reminder that redemption often emerges from the depths of pain. In Rom 5:8 Paul writes, "But God demonstrates his own love for us in this: While we were still sinners, Christ died for us." This verse illustrates that God's love is most evident in our brokenness. Through Christ's suffering, we are invited to participate in a transformative relationship with him, one that acknowledges our pain and despair while offering the promise of hope and renewal. The act of suffering becomes a means through which we can experience God's grace, allowing us to grow spiritually and develop resilience in the face of adversity. In our moments of weakness, we often find ourselves relying more fully on God's strength, discovering that his grace is sufficient (2 Cor 12:9). This reliance can foster a deeper intimacy with God as we learn to lean on him in times of trouble.

Furthermore, suffering has a unique way of uniting believers in their faith journey. When Christians face trials, they often find strength in community and the shared experience of seeking God's presence amid hardship. As Henri Nouwen reflects in *The Wounded Healer*, "The great illusion of leadership is to think that man can be led out of the desert by someone who has never been there."[9] This quote underscores the importance of shared suffering as a pathway to healing and understanding. In our struggles, we not only discover our need for God but also realize the depth of connection we share with others who have faced similar challenges. Together, we can bear one another's burdens, embodying the love and compassion of Christ in tangible ways. The church, in this context, becomes a sanctuary where shared stories of pain can lead to mutual encouragement, reminding us that we are not alone in our struggles and that healing often comes through relationships built on vulnerability and honesty.

Ultimately, suffering can lead us to a deeper understanding of God's redemptive work in our lives. The cross stands as a testament to the reality that God brings good out of suffering, weaving

---

9. Nouwen, *Wounded Healer*, 51.

together our stories of pain into a narrative of hope. As we navigate our own suffering, we can hold on to the assurance that God is continually at work, transforming our trials into opportunities for growth, healing, and renewed faith. In this process, we can become instruments of his grace to others, extending comfort to those who suffer as we have been comforted (2 Cor 1:4). Thus, suffering not only has the potential to deepen our relationship with God but also empowers us to serve others in their pain, demonstrating the very heart of the gospel.

Conclusion

While we may never fully answer the question of why bad things happen to good people, we can find solace in the assurance that God is intimately present in our suffering. Scripture reminds us that suffering is a temporary condition, a part of our earthly existence that ultimately serves a greater purpose. In Rom 8:18 Paul writes, "I consider that our present sufferings are not worth comparing with the glory that will be revealed in us." This verse encapsulates the Christian hope that transcends our immediate circumstances, urging us to look beyond our pain and toward God's promise of restoration and redemption.

Throughout the Bible, we see a consistent theme of God's faithfulness amid human suffering. From Job's trials to Christ's anguish in the garden of Gethsemane, we witness how God does not shy away from our pain but instead enters into it with us. His presence in our suffering is not only a comfort but a testament to his deep love for humanity. As we reflect on the life and ministry of Jesus, we see that he embraced suffering not as a detour from his mission but as an integral part of it. His willingness to endure pain and injustice underscores the depth of God's commitment to our redemption.

Moreover, our understanding of suffering can be transformed when we recognize that it often catalyzes spiritual growth and deeper faith. As we navigate the trials of life, we are called to lean on God's promises and trust that his purposes, though often hidden, are good. In Jer 29:11 God assures us, "For I know the plans I have for you," plans that are not meant to harm us but to give us hope and a future. This promise is a powerful reminder that even when we cannot see the path ahead, God orchestrates our lives with intentionality and love.

In times of suffering, we are also called to support one another within the community of faith. The New Testament encourages believers to bear one another's burdens (Gal 6:2), fostering an environment of compassion and understanding. Our shared experiences of suffering can forge deep connections and create opportunities for healing as we walk alongside one another in our struggles. This communal aspect of faith reminds us that we are not alone; God has equipped us with a community of believers to uplift and encourage us during our darkest hours.

Ultimately, the Christian narrative offers us a profound perspective on suffering. Rather than viewing it as an insurmountable obstacle, we can embrace it as part of our journey toward deeper intimacy with God. The cross stands as a symbol of hope, illustrating that suffering can lead to transformation and renewal. In Christ, we find the promise that our pain is not wasted; it is woven into the tapestry of God's redemptive story.

As we conclude our exploration of suffering and its relationship to faith, let us hold fast to the assurance that God is with us in our pain. We may not understand the reasons behind our suffering, but we can trust his goodness and sovereignty. Ultimately, we are reminded that our suffering is not the final word; God's promise of restoration and redemption ultimately prevails, inviting us to experience his grace and love in profound ways.

Application

Take a moment to reflect on a difficult time in your life when you struggled with the question of why bad things happen to good people. Think back to those moments of pain, uncertainty, or injustice. What emotions did you experience? Did anger, confusion, or sadness accompany your questions about God's goodness in the face of suffering? Reconciling such experiences with faith can often be a challenging journey. However, it can also lead to profound growth and deeper understanding.

Consider how you navigated your thoughts and feelings during that difficult time. Did you find solace in prayer, Scripture, or the support of your community? Reflecting on the story of Job, who endured unimaginable suffering yet remained steadfast in his faith, can provide valuable insights. Despite not receiving the answers he sought, Job's unwavering trust in God serves as a powerful example of how faith can withstand the fiercest storms. How might you embody Job's resilience and trust in your life, especially when facing inexplicable trials?

Similarly, the teachings of Jesus offer a lens through which we can view suffering. Jesus, who suffered greatly for our sake, demonstrated that pain does not diminish God's love for us. When he cried out in anguish on the cross, "My God, my God, why have you forsaken me?" (Matt 27:46), he embraced the depths of human suffering, showing that questioning God is part of the faith journey. Reflect on how acknowledging your pain and confusion, just as Jesus did, can lead you to a more authentic relationship with God.

As you consider these lessons, think about the role of trust in your spiritual life. How might trusting in God's sovereignty help you find peace amid hardship? While we may not understand why certain events unfold, believing God is in control can provide comfort and reassurance. Accepting the limits of your understanding can liberate you from the burden of trying to have all the answers. Instead of wrestling with "why," you can focus on "who"—the God who walks with you through your suffering, who promises to be your refuge and strength (Ps 46:1).

In practical terms, how can you apply these reflections to your current circumstances? Perhaps it involves seeking support from a faith community, engaging in prayer or meditation, or immersing yourself in Scripture to find encouragement and strength. You might also consider reaching out to someone who is currently experiencing suffering, offering them a listening ear or sharing your own journey. By doing so, you not only honor your own experiences but also become a source of comfort and hope for others, which is a powerful way to live out your faith.

Ultimately, allowing the lessons of Joseph and Jesus to influence your response to suffering can lead to a more profound understanding of God's presence in your life. Embrace the journey, knowing that even in the darkest valleys, you are not alone. Your faith can be a source of strength, guiding you toward peace, healing, and renewed hope.

Reflection Questions

1. Personal experience: Reflect on a challenging time in your life when you grappled with the question of why bad things happen to good people. What emotions did you experience, and how did these feelings impact your faith in God?

2. Lessons from Scripture: How can the lessons from Job's perseverance and Jesus's suffering provide insight into your own experiences? Identify specific teachings that resonate with you and discuss how they can be applied in your current situation.

3. Trust and understanding: How can trusting in God's sovereignty and accepting the limits of your understanding lead to peace during difficult times? Reflect on biblical passages or personal anecdotes that illustrate this trust.

4. Community support: How can you seek or provide support within your faith community during times of suffering? Consider ways you can engage with others who are experiencing hardships, using your experiences to offer hope.

Closing Prayer

Lord, we come before you with heavy hearts, seeking to understand why we endure suffering, especially when it feels so undeserved.

Remind us of your unwavering love and perfect sovereignty in moments of confusion and pain. Help us trust that you are with us in every trial, assuring us that we are never abandoned, even when the reasons for our suffering remain hidden.

May your presence comfort us in our darkest hours, and may we find peace in the assurance that you have a greater plan for our lives—one filled with hope and redemption. Strengthen our faith in times of doubt and empower us to walk in your light, trusting that you are good and faithful, even when our circumstances say otherwise.

As we leave this space, may we carry with us the lessons learned and the hope found in you. Help us to share that hope with others who are suffering, reflecting your love in our words and actions. In Jesus's name, we pray. Amen.

CHAPTER 7

The Need to Grieve

*The Lord is close to the brokenhearted
and saves those who are crushed in spirit.*

—Psalm 34:18

Introduction: Why We Must Grieve

Grief is an unavoidable part of life, yet it is often something we try to avoid or rush through. In today's fast-paced world, societal pressure encourages us to quickly move on from losses, to push through the pain, and to suppress emotions that may make others—and sometimes ourselves—uncomfortable. Phrases like "stay strong" or "get over it" suggest that lingering in grief is a weakness or failure to cope. However, this view ignores the essential role grief plays in our emotional and spiritual well-being.

Theologically, grief is not an indication of faithlessness, but rather, a natural and necessary response to loss. The Bible offers numerous examples of grieving. The Psalms, for example, are filled with laments expressing profound sorrow, showing us how to cry out to God in our deepest pain (Ps 13:1–2). Even Jesus wept at the tomb of his friend Lazarus, demonstrating that grief has a place in the journey of faith (John 11:35). Far from hindering our faith, grief can deepen our trust and reliance on God, the ultimate source of comfort (2 Cor 1:3–4).

Granger E. Westberg's *Good Grief* emphasizes that grief is not a weakness but a vital process for healing. He notes that unresolved grief can lead to emotional difficulties such as bitterness or depression.[1] By avoiding grief, we risk carrying pain that may resurface in harmful ways. As Westberg suggests, we must allow ourselves to move through grief intentionally, allowing it to guide us toward healing. Similarly, Elisabeth Kübler-Ross asserts that embracing grief helps individuals come to terms with their loss instead of denying it.[2]

In Christian spirituality, grief is an invitation to draw closer to God. According to C. S. Lewis, grief is not something to hide from God, but a space to wrestle with our pain in his presence. He writes, "No one ever told me that grief felt so like fear . . . I am not afraid, but the sensation is like being afraid. The same fluttering in the stomach, the same restlessness."[3] This vivid portrayal captures the intensity of grief, but also points to the truth that God meets us in our sorrow. When we allow ourselves to grieve, we create space for God to offer his comfort and healing.

Avoiding grief denies us the opportunity to experience God's healing presence. Instead of rushing past sorrow, we are invited to bring our whole selves before God—tears, doubts, and all. This chapter will explore the necessity of grieving emotionally and spiritually. Far from being a sign of weakness, grief is a transformative process leading us to wholeness. By embracing it, we open ourselves to encounter God in our sorrow, trusting that he is near to the brokenhearted (Ps 34:18).

---

1. Westberg, *Good Grief*, 12–14.
2. Kübler-Ross and Kessler, *On Grief and Grieving*, 7.
3. Lewis, *Grief Observed*, 5.

Grief in the Bible: A Godly Response to Loss

The Bible is full of examples of people who grieved deeply and openly. Far from being condemned for their sadness, they were often met with God's comfort and presence. One of the most striking examples is Jesus himself, who wept at the tomb of his friend Lazarus. Even though he knew he was about to raise Lazarus from the dead, Jesus still took time to mourn. In John 11:35, the shortest verse in the Bible, we see the depth of Jesus's humanity: "Jesus wept." This moment reveals that grief is not something to be rushed through or avoided. If the Son of God could fully enter into grief, so can we.

Other biblical figures, like David, also provide profound examples of grief. When David's son with Bathsheba was ill, he fasted and wept for days (2 Sam 12:16). After learning that the child had died, he worshipped, acknowledging that his mourning had brought him closer to God. The Psalms are filled with David's laments, showing us that crying out to God in our pain is acceptable and an act of faith. In these cries, David models how to grieve in a way that keeps us connected to God rather than turning away in bitterness.

Job is another classic example of grief in the face of unimaginable loss. After losing his children, wealth, and health, Job did not suppress his emotions. He expressed his anguish openly, questioning God and lamenting his suffering. However, through this process, he remained in dialogue with God, and ultimately, his faith was deepened. As Burton Z. Cooper argues in *Why God?*, Job's story illustrates the theological concept of divine hiddenness and how grief can lead to deeper trust in God despite his silence.[4] Job's story reminds us that grief is not a sign of a lack of faith; it is a way to remain engaged with God in our darkest moments.

In addition to these examples, we can look to the prophet Jeremiah, often called the weeping prophet, as another vivid portrait of godly grief. Jeremiah's deep sorrow over Jerusalem's impending destruction and his people's suffering is expressed throughout the

---

4. Cooper, *Why God?*, 45–47.

book of Lamentations, where he pours out his lament to God. In Lam 3 Jeremiah's grief is palpable: "I am the man who has seen affliction by the rod of Lord's wrath. He ... has broken my bones" (Lam 3:1-4). Yet, amid his deep lamentation, Jeremiah finds hope, proclaiming, "Yet this I call to mind and therefore I have hope: Because of the Lord's great love we are not consumed, for his compassions never fail" (Lam 3:21-22). This duality of sorrow and hope shows us that grieving before God can lead us to a profound recognition of his unending mercy and faithfulness, even in the darkest times. Nicholas Wolterstorff suggests that grief often deepens our understanding of the divine: "In the valley of suffering, despair and bitterness are brewed. But there also character is made. The valley of suffering is the vale of soul-making."[5] Grieving before God is not a detour away from faith but a crucial part of the journey toward healing and transformation.

Why Grief Matters: Spiritual and Emotional Healing

Grief is not only an emotional response but also a transformative journey toward healing and wholeness. It strips away the illusions of control, reminding us of our vulnerability and dependence on God. In moments of loss, we often confront profound questions about life, purpose, and the nature of God, unveiling our need for connection and reassurance from our Creator. When we allow ourselves to grieve, we create a sacred space where God meets us in our brokenness. The Bible reassures us in Ps 34:18, "The Lord is close to the brokenhearted and saves those who are crushed in spirit," reminding us that even in sorrow, we are not alone. God's presence envelops us, offering comfort and hope amid despair.

From a psychological perspective, suppressing grief can lead to more severe emotional and physical consequences, such as depression or anxiety. Granger E. Westberg, explains that avoiding grief often results in feelings of numbness and disconnection.

---

5. Wolterstorff, *Lament for a Son*, 34.

In contrast, confronting grief allows for healing and acceptance.[6] Judith Lewis Herman underscores the importance of expressing grief, suggesting that healing comes when we recount our painful experiences, affirming that grief is a healthy, necessary response to loss.[7]

Grief also invites spiritual growth. In times of profound sorrow, we often seek God more earnestly, deepening our relationship with him. Burton Z. Cooper, in *Why God?*, discusses how grief can lead to spiritual resilience. He writes that grappling with God's silence during suffering can deepen our faith, encouraging us to seek God even in our darkest moments.[8] Grief, rather than weakening our faith, can become a catalyst for growth, drawing us closer to God and transforming our understanding of his nature.

Furthermore, grief is not a solitary journey. Romans 12:15 reminds us to "rejoice with those who rejoice; mourn with those who mourn." God designed us for community, and sharing our grief with others fosters healing. In *The Grief Recovery Handbook*, John W. James and Russell Friedman highlight that bearing one another's burdens within a community promotes connection and emotional recovery.[9] The support of others not only provides comfort but also creates opportunities for shared vulnerability, reinforcing that we do not need to carry our burdens alone.

This shared grief fosters empathy and compassion, strengthening our relationships with others and with God. Henri Nouwen, in *The Wounded Healer*, writes that our wounds can become sources of healing for others, empowering us to minister to one another through our own experiences of loss.[10]

Ultimately, embracing grief opens pathways to spiritual and emotional growth. Acknowledging our pain invites God's healing presence, moving us from brokenness to wholeness. Understanding grief as an integral part of the human experience allows it to

---

6. Westberg, *Good Grief*, 23.
7. Herman, *Trauma and Recovery*, 175.
8. Cooper, *Why God?*, 52.
9. James and Friedman, *Grief Recovery Handbook*, 63.
10. Nouwen, *Wounded Healer*, 45.

shape us, cultivating resilience and deepening our faith in the God who walks with us through our darkest valleys.

Biblical Principles for Grieving in a Godly Way

Grieving in a godly way does not mean suppressing emotions or rushing to find the silver lining. Instead, it involves being honest with God and trusting that he is present in our sorrow. The Bible provides several principles for grieving in a way that honors God and brings us closer to him.

First, we are called to be honest with God in our pain. The Psalms, especially those written by David, are filled with raw emotion and vulnerability. David never hesitates to express his fears, doubts, or anger. For example, Ps 13 begins with a poignant cry: "How long, Lord? Will you forget me forever? How long will you hide your face from me?" This candid expression of despair sets the stage for a heartfelt dialogue with God. By the end of the psalm, David turns back to praise, declaring, "But I trust in your unfailing love; my heart rejoices in your salvation" (v. 5). This progression demonstrates that we can trust God's goodness and faithfulness even in grief. Embracing this honesty not only deepens our relationship with God but also acknowledges the reality of our emotional landscape, which can be an essential step in the healing process.

Second, we must remember that grief is not the absence of hope. The apostle Paul reminds us in 1 Thess 4:13 that while we grieve, we do not do so "like the rest of mankind, who have no hope." The resurrection of Jesus Christ serves as the ultimate assurance that death is not the end but rather a transition to eternal life. This hope allows us to navigate our grief, knowing that God's promises are greater than our pain. When we grieve with hope, we are empowered to honor the memories of those we have lost while still looking forward to the fulfillment of God's promises. This perspective transforms our mourning into a process of remembrance and celebration rather than mere sorrow. It encourages us to see our grief as part of a larger narrative of redemption, in which God is actively working in our lives even amid heartache.

Third, we must lean into the process of lament. Lament is a biblical practice that acknowledges our pain while maintaining faith in God's ultimate redemption. In *A Grief Observed*, C. S. Lewis reflects on how grief can drive us to deeper faith, even when we feel abandoned by God. He writes, "God whispers to us in our pleasures, speaks in our conscience, but shouts in our pains: It is his megaphone to rouse a deaf world."[11] Lament allows us to voice our grief while still holding onto faith, inviting God into our struggles and doubts. This process is not merely a onetime event but a journey that unfolds over time. The act of lament can be cathartic, allowing us to articulate our suffering and seek understanding and comfort from God.

Moreover, lament can foster a deeper connection among believers (Rom 12:15). When we share our grief within the context of community, we not only receive support but also strengthen our bonds with others. This mutual sharing creates an environment where vulnerability is accepted and encourages healing as we bear one another's burdens. Grieving in community can provide opportunities for accountability, prayer, and encouragement, reminding us that we are not alone in our sorrow.

Finally, it is essential to remember that grief is a process that varies for each individual. Just as Jesus wept at the tomb of Lazarus, showing us the importance of mourning (John 11:35), we, too, must recognize that everyone grieves differently. Some may need more time to process their emotions, while others may find solace in serving others or engaging in worship. Honoring our unique grieving process—and allowing others to do the same—can facilitate a more compassionate understanding of how to support one another in times of loss.

Ultimately, these principles guide us in navigating our grief in a manner that honors God. They remind us that while grief is painful, it is also an opportunity for profound spiritual growth and a deeper connection with our Creator. Embracing honesty, hope,

---

11. Lewis, *Grief Observed*, 81.

lament, and community can lead us through the valley of sorrow into a place of healing and renewed faith. By doing so, we not only honor the memories of those we have lost but also open ourselves to the transformative power of God's love, which meets us in our brokenness and promises restoration.

How to Grieve in a Healthy Way: Insights from Experts

Grieving is a profoundly individual experience, yet it is also a universal human response to loss. Though each person's grief is unique, many experts and theologians agree on essential strategies for navigating grief healthily—ways that promote both emotional and spiritual healing. A holistic approach to grief can be formed by combining insights from psychology, biblical teachings, and counseling. The guidance offered by these professionals emphasizes the need for emotional expression, community support, spiritual discipline, and professional intervention when necessary.

1. Allow Yourself to Express Emotions

A healthy grieving process begins with allowing oneself to feel and express emotions. Experts like Elisabeth Kübler-Ross, known for her groundbreaking work on the five stages of grief, advocate for emotional transparency in the grieving process. Kübler-Ross emphasizes that denial, anger, bargaining, depression, and acceptance are all natural responses to loss, and experiencing them openly is crucial to finding healing.[12] Suppressing emotions, by contrast, can lead to emotional blockages that prevent individuals from moving forward, resulting in prolonged suffering or unresolved grief.

Psychologists and theologians highlight that emotional expression—whether through crying, talking, or other creative outlets—is essential to the healing process. In *Good Grief*, Granger E. Westberg underlines the importance of emotional honesty,

---

12. Kübler-Ross and Kessler, *On Grief and Grieving*, 32–33.

explaining that individuals who suppress grief are more likely to experience feelings of detachment, numbness, and depression.[13] The Bible, too, encourages us to express grief openly. Jesus himself expressed raw emotion, as seen in John 11:35, where "Jesus wept." His tears over Lazarus's death remind us that grieving is not only natural but a part of our human experience, even as we hold onto faith.

2. Engage in Community Support

While grief often leads to withdrawal, isolating oneself can amplify feelings of despair. Engaging with others is a crucial aspect of healthy grieving. Grief researcher Alan D. Wolfelt emphasizes that humans are inherently social beings, and community support plays a vital role in the healing process.[14] Wolfelt explains that grieving individuals benefit from sharing their burden with others, whether in faith communities, family settings, or support groups.[15] The Bible echoes this, urging believers to "mourn with those who mourn" (Rom 12:15), underscoring the need for mutual empathy and support during times of loss.

In Christian communities, this support can often come from small groups, pastors, and friends who walk alongside the grieving, providing not only practical help but spiritual encouragement. Nancy Guthrie explains that God often works through others to provide comfort in times of grief.[16] She encourages the grieving to remain connected to their church and community, where they can find shared strength and experience the healing presence of God through the love and prayers of others.

3. Practice Spiritual Disciplines

Theologians and grief counselors agree that incorporating spiritual practices like prayer, meditation, and Scripture reading is vital to the healing process. During times of grief, these disciplines

---

13. Westberg, *Good Grief*, 26–27.
14. Wolfelt, *Journey Through Grief*, 44–45.
15. Wolfelt, *Journey Through Grief*, 94.
16. Guthrie, *Hearing Jesus Speak*, 61.

help individuals anchor their emotions in God's promises. J. Todd Billings, in *Rejoicing in Lament*, reflects on how lamentation—pouring out sorrow before God—can be a transformative spiritual practice that invites divine healing.[17] Lament is not simply a cry of despair, but a way of voicing grief while maintaining trust in God's faithfulness.

Incorporating Scripture is another powerful means of healing. Verses like Ps 34:18, "The Lord is close to the brokenhearted and saves those who are crushed in spirit," remind the grieving of God's presence during their darkest moments. Meditation on such passages can bring comfort and provide a means to process grief within the broader context of God's redemptive plan. Spiritual disciplines also encourage introspection, helping individuals to discern how God might be using their grief for spiritual growth, as C. S. Lewis observed in *A Grief Observed*: "God whispers to us in our pleasures, speaks in our conscience, but shouts in our pains: It is his megaphone to rouse a deaf world."[18]

4. Seek Professional Help if Needed

For many individuals, grief may require professional help. Christian counselors and therapists offer specialized care, integrating biblical truths with therapeutic approaches. When grief becomes overwhelming or complicated by other mental health concerns, such as anxiety, depression, or trauma, professional intervention can provide much-needed guidance. Burton Z. Cooper argues that professional counseling can assist individuals in reconciling their faith with their grief, helping them make sense of their loss while fostering spiritual and emotional growth.[19]

In addition to traditional therapy, faith-based grief support groups such as GriefShare can provide a communal environment where participants are encouraged to process their grief alongside others who share their faith. These groups often provide a safe space for prayer, shared stories, and mutual encouragement.

17. Billings, *Rejoicing in Lament*, 103.
18. Lewis, *Grief Observed*, 81.
19. Cooper, *Why God?*, 67.

Christian counselors like H. Norman Wright also advocate using practical tools such as journaling and cognitive behavioral techniques to reframe negative thinking patterns, guiding individuals toward hope and healing.[20]

5. Engage in Self-Care and Balance

Finally, caring for oneself physically, emotionally, and spiritually is vital to the grieving process. Grief affects the whole person, and neglecting one's health can exacerbate feelings of hopelessness and exhaustion. Experts like Elisabeth Kübler-Ross encourage grievers to engage in self-care practices such as regular exercise, sufficient rest, and healthy eating.[21] Beyond physical care, integrating practices like mindfulness and prayerful reflection can help ground individuals in the present moment, reducing anxiety and fostering emotional resilience.

Self-care also includes setting boundaries with others and engaging in personal activities that bring joy and peace, such as reading, walking, or hobbies. C. S. Lewis reminds readers that grief is not something that can be rushed, and allowing oneself to grieve in their own time is vital to healing.[22] Grief is cyclical, often returning in waves, but attending to personal health can provide the strength to weather those emotional tides

The Gift of Grief: A Path to Deeper Faith

Grief, while undoubtedly painful, holds within it the potential to lead us to a deeper and more mature faith. As we face sorrow, we encounter our human limitations, and this very vulnerability is where God's strength can shine through. In 2 Cor 12:9 Paul teaches, "My grace is sufficient for you, for my power is made perfect in weakness." In times of grief, we are reminded that we cannot rely on our own strength. Instead, these moments present opportunities

---

20. Wright, *Complete Guide*, 88.
21. Kübler-Ross and Kessler, *On Grief and Grieving*, 85–86.
22. Lewis, *Grief Observed*, 9.

to surrender our pain to God and allow his grace to sustain us. This reliance on divine strength is one of the profound ways grief becomes a gift, drawing us closer to the heart of God.

Grief often brings with it moments of doubt, confusion, and questioning. However, many theologians emphasize that this struggle is not a sign of a lack of faith but rather a deepening process. J. Todd Billings writes in *Rejoicing in Lament*, "Through lament, we discover that our faith is not about always having the right answers but about trusting in the God who is faithful to us, even when our lives fall apart."[23] As Christians lament, they can cling to the promise that God is present in their suffering and is capable of transforming that pain into spiritual growth. This idea reflects a profound biblical truth—grief refines and purifies our faith, much like how fire refines gold (1 Pet 1:7).

In *A Grief Observed*, C. S. Lewis also noted how grief can become a tool for deepening our faith: "You never know how much you really believe anything until its truth or falsehood becomes a matter of life and death to you."[24] Grief forces believers to confront the core of their faith and reevaluate their understanding of God. Through this process, believers may discover a more resilient and profound trust in God's sovereignty and love.

By allowing ourselves to grieve, we open ourselves to the transforming power of God's grace. Rather than resisting pain, embracing it within the context of faith can lead to healing. Theologian Henri Nouwen explains that "the wounds we most fear are often the ones through which God's grace most powerfully flows."[25] In grief, believers experience a profound brokenness that allows them to experience God's grace, as he gently tends to their wounds and strengthens their faith.

Grieving in faith shifts the focus from human weakness to divine power. As we acknowledge our helplessness, we provide God with the space to work in ways that transcend our understanding. It is in this surrender, where we lay our grief before God, that his

---

23. Billings, *Rejoicing in Lament*, 89.
24. Lewis, *Grief Observed*, 38.
25. Nouwen, *Wounded Healer*, 47.

grace sustains us, as Paul himself experienced. This kind of spiritual surrender allows God to bring restoration to the deepest parts of our hearts.

Another dimension of grief is its ability to remind believers of the eternal hope found in Christ. The promise of resurrection softens the pain of loss. As Paul reminds us in 1 Thess 4:13, we "do not grieve like the rest of mankind, who have no hope." The resurrection of Jesus Christ is the ultimate assurance that death is not the final word. This truth allows Christians to face grief with an eternal perspective, knowing that life continues beyond this earthly existence. The promise of eternal life with God becomes the anchor that holds believers firm even in their deepest sorrows.

N. T. Wright, in *Surprised by Hope*, reflects on how Christian hope is tied directly to the resurrection: "The point of the resurrection . . . is that the present bodily life is not valueless just because it will die. . . . What you do with your body in the present matters because God has a great future in store for it."[26] This assurance of a future resurrection infuses grief with hope, transforming it from mere sadness into an anticipation of God's ultimate victory over death and pain. The grieving process, therefore, becomes not just a moment of loss but a space for the believer to cling to the eternal promises of God.

Grief, while intensely personal, also has a communal dimension. Within the Christian faith, believers are called to grieve alongside one another. Paul's command in Rom 12:15, "Rejoice with those who rejoice; mourn with those who mourn," highlights the importance of shared grief in the body of Christ. Through community, grief is not only a personal journey but a collective experience that strengthens the faith of the entire group. God's presence is often felt most profoundly in this shared grieving, as he works through others to comfort and support.

Grief shared with a faith community creates a space for collective healing and restoration. In *Life Together*, Dietrich Bonhoeffer speaks to the importance of communal faith in times of suffering: "The Christian needs another Christian who speaks God's Word

---

26. Wright, *Surprised by Hope*, 208.

to him. He needs him again and again when he becomes uncertain and discouraged."[27] In this light, grief becomes a sacred space for the body of Christ to function as God's hands and feet, offering support and encouragement to one another.

Conclusion: Embracing the Need to Grieve

Grieving is not a sign of weakness or a lack of faith but an essential part of the human experience. Both the Bible and theological reflections show that grief is not something to avoid but to embrace. The grieving process is an invitation from God to encounter his comfort and healing. As we navigate our sorrow, we are reminded that God is with us, present in our pain and offering his peace.

The act of grieving gives us a deeper understanding of our dependence on God. As J. Todd Billings notes, "Grief and lament allow us to realize our vulnerability and open us to the transformative work of Christ."[28] Billings's reflections on his battle with cancer illustrate how grief strips away illusions of control, leading us to greater reliance on God's grace. Similarly, C. S. Lewis emphasizes how grieving can feel like fear, but it also reminds us of the fragility of life and the profound depth of divine love.[29]

The Psalms, especially the lament psalms, offer a biblical framework for grieving. David's cries to God in his moments of despair illustrate that lament is an act of faith, not of doubt. As Dietrich Bonhoeffer explains, "In lament, we lay bare our hearts before God, acknowledging our need for His presence and help."[30] In grieving, we express our deepest pains, trusting that God is near to the brokenhearted, as Scripture promises (Ps 34:18).

Ultimately, embracing grief leads us toward healing, both emotionally and spiritually. It reminds us that sorrow is not the end of the story, as N. T. Wright confirms: "Grief, for the Christian,

---

27. Bonhoeffer, *Life Together*, 23.
28. Billings, *Rejoicing in Lament*, 54.
29. Lewis, *Grief Observed*, 23.
30. Bonhoeffer, *Life Together*, 32.

is always tinged with hope because of the resurrection of Jesus."[31] This hope does not erase our grief but offers a foundation upon which we can face even the deepest losses.

By walking through grief, we open ourselves to God's restorative work, trusting that his power is made perfect in our weakness (2 Cor 12:9). In these moments of vulnerability, we find God's strength carrying us through. Grief is not just an emotional process; it is a spiritual journey that draws us closer to the heart of God and his promise of new life in Christ.

Application

As you reflect on your experiences with grief, consider how embracing the process of mourning can lead to spiritual and emotional healing rather than rushing through or suppressing it. Scripture teaches us that lamenting and being honest with our emotions allows God's presence to meet us in our pain. Practically, this can be applied in several important ways.

Allow Space for Emotion

Grieving is not something to avoid or suppress. Allowing yourself to feel the pain and sorrow that comes with loss is essential to the healing process. As Jesus wept at the tomb of Lazarus (John 11:35), we see that even he allowed room for deep, emotional expression. Grieving is not a sign of weakness but an acknowledgment of the reality of loss. As C. S. Lewis writes in *A Grief Observed*, "No one ever told me that grief felt so like fear. . . . I am not afraid, but the sensation is like being afraid."[32] This vulnerability opens us to experience God's comfort and presence.

---

31. Wright, *Surprised by Hope*, 74.
32. Lewis, *Grief Observed*, 4.

Turn to Scripture and Prayer

In times of grief, turning to Scripture provides comfort and perspective. Biblical figures like David, Job, and even Jesus modeled how to bring deep sorrow before God. Psalm 42, for instance, captures David's longing for God in his distress: "My tears have been my food day and night" (v. 3). Likewise, Job's lamentation in the face of unimaginable loss offers an example of how to process grief while still trusting God's sovereignty (Job 3). Even when words fail, engaging in prayer creates space for God's healing touch. Granger E. Westberg suggests that "faithful lament offers a space where we can be most honest with God, trusting that he can handle our pain."[33]

Grieve in Community

We are not meant to bear grief alone. The Bible calls us to "mourn with those who mourn" (Rom 12:15), recognizing the value of shared sorrow within the body of Christ. When we grieve together, we remind each other of God's presence and hope. In *Life Together*, Dietrich Bonhoeffer explains the significance of community in times of sorrow, noting that "bearing one another's burdens fulfills the law of Christ."[34] By opening ourselves up to others, we receive comfort, support, and companionship that can be instrumental in our healing journey.

Seek Professional Help if Needed

Grief can be overwhelming, and sometimes professional help is necessary to process it in a healthy way. Christian counselors and therapists can provide biblically grounded strategies to work through grief, ensuring that emotions are not suppressed but dealt

---

33. Westberg, *Good Grief*, 21.
34. Bonhoeffer, *Life Together*, 72.

with in ways that promote healing. In *The Wounded Healer*, Henri Nouwen suggests that seeking help from trained professionals can guide individuals to integrate their faith with their emotional pain, fostering deeper spiritual growth.[35] Burton Z. Cooper also emphasizes the importance of reconciling grief with faith, noting that counseling can offer much-needed tools for navigating loss while deepening one's relationship with God.[36]

Reflection Questions

1. How have I personally handled grief in the past? Have I been open with my emotions, or have I suppressed them to avoid discomfort?
2. What biblical examples of grief resonate with me the most? How can I apply their stories to my own experiences of loss?
3. In what ways have I leaned on my community during times of mourning? How can I offer support to others in their grief?
4. How can I invite God into my grieving process in a deeper way?

Closing Prayer

Heavenly Father, you are the God of all comfort, and you walk with us through every season of life. In times of grief and loss, help us to turn to you and lean on your strength. Teach us to grieve in a way that brings us closer to you, embracing our pain with the assurance that you are present with us. We trust in your promise to heal the brokenhearted and bind up our wounds, knowing that your grace is sufficient. May our grief deepen our reliance on you and bring us closer to the hope we have in Christ. In Jesus's name, we pray. Amen.

---

35. Nouwen, *Wounded Healer*, 15.
36. Cooper, *Why God?*, 67.

CHAPTER 8

Seeing God Through the Tears

Introduction: The Divine Encounter in Grief

As we conclude our exploration of grief and healing, it becomes evident that tears are not just an outward reflection of sorrow but an intimate invitation to encounter God's presence. Grief, in its rawest form, draws us into a place where we can meet God in profound ways. Scripture repeatedly shows that God is not distant from our pain but is near, deeply empathetic, and intimately involved in our suffering. In Ps 56:8 we are reminded that God collects every tear in a bottle, a powerful image of his attentiveness and care. The tears we shed are sacred; they represent not only our suffering but also our openness to God's healing presence.

Grief is an invitation to lay down the weight of our pain at God's feet. In Matt 11:28 Jesus declares, "Come to me, all you who are weary and burdened, and I will give you rest." This promise speaks directly to those in the midst of grief, offering a divine rest that is not devoid of suffering but one where God actively participates in our emotional and spiritual restoration. Grief can break us open in ways that allow for a deeper experience of God's love and compassion. In these moments of vulnerability, we find a fresh understanding of his heart for us.

This final chapter reflects on the key lessons learned through the stories of Job, Jonah, Samson, and Hezekiah and our personal journeys. These biblical figures experienced grief, loss, and frustration, but through their struggles, they encountered God's transformative grace. As we revisit these stories, we see how grief, though painful, serves as a conduit to greater spiritual depth, renewal, and intimacy with God.

When we allow ourselves to embrace grief, we invite God into our deepest wounds. The paradox is that in our sorrow, we also find strength, as God uses our brokenness to bring healing. In 2 Cor 12:9 Paul reminds us of this truth: "My grace is sufficient for you, for my power is made perfect in weakness." In our most fragile state, we encounter God's strength in ways we could not have known otherwise.

Grief ultimately leads us to transformation. It is a journey where the soul is reshaped, our perspectives shift, and we learn to trust God's goodness, even when life feels uncertain. In this chapter, we will explore how grief can be a path to a deeper, more intimate relationship with God as we lean into his promises, his comfort, and his enduring presence.

The Purpose of Grief: A Transformative Process

Grief, while painful, serves a critical purpose in our spiritual and emotional lives. It is a necessary process that allows us to open ourselves to God's healing and restoration. Grief often feels like a heavy burden, yet within that burden lies an opportunity for deep spiritual growth. As we explored in chapter 1 with Job, worship plays a vital role in navigating grief. When Job faced the loss of everything he held dear, his first response was to fall to the ground in worship (Job 1:20). Yet, it is crucial to note that the first thing the enemy targeted was Job's ability to worship—his oxen and flocks, the very means of offering sacrifices. The enemy will always attempt to disrupt our worship in moments of pain. However, Job's unwavering devotion, even in the face of unimaginable loss, teaches us that worship strengthens our connection to God during our darkest hours. Through grief, we find that worship helps us realign our hearts with God, shifting our focus from suffering to his sustaining presence.

This act of worship is not about ignoring the pain but acknowledging God's sovereignty within it. Job's journey reminds us that in grief, we learn to rely on God's strength rather than our own. These vulnerable moments open us up to fully experience God's sustaining power. The more we pour out our grief to God, the more we receive his comfort, peace, and strength.

In John 11:35 we witness Jesus himself weeping at the death of Lazarus. His tears demonstrate divine empathy, showing that grief is not something to avoid or suppress. Jesus did not dismiss the pain of those mourning Lazarus but entered into their grief, feeling it deeply. His tears highlight the profound truth that God is not only aware of our suffering but is also moved by it. Jesus's tears underscore that grief is an essential part of the human experience and a necessary process for emotional and spiritual healing.

In chapter 3, Samson's story offers a unique perspective on how unchecked grief can impact our lives, leading to destructive patterns fueled by unresolved emotions. Samson experienced profound personal loss and disappointment, most notably through his relationships and betrayals, which triggered a deep sense of grief. However, instead of processing his pain in a healthy way, Samson allowed it to fester, channeling it into anger, bitterness, and a desire for vengeance. His grief, unresolved and unchecked, drove him to act impulsively, often using his immense strength not for God's purposes but to satisfy his own emotional needs.

This self-driven response illustrates how grief can become a gateway for misguided actions when we do not seek God's guidance. Samson's story exemplifies the danger of allowing grief to control us, leading us down paths that harm both ourselves and others. His grief over lost relationships and unmet expectations caused him to lose sight of his divine calling, steering him into cycles of retaliation and destruction.

Despite Samson's flawed response, God's redemptive grace remained at work in his life. Even amid his failures, God's plan for Samson was never derailed. At the end of his life, Samson called out to God one final time, asking for strength for the fulfillment of God's purposes (Judg 16:28). This moment reflects a shift in

Samson's heart, where, even in his brokenness, he recognized his need for God.

Samson's life is a powerful reminder that even when grief leads us astray, God's mercy and grace offer a path to redemption. His story emphasizes the importance of seeking God's purposes over our own when we are grieving. Grief, if not surrendered to God, can lead us into spiritual darkness, causing us to make decisions that deviate from his will. However, no matter how far we stray, God provides opportunities to realign our hearts and actions with his divine intentions.

Key Insight

Grief can transform our relationship with God, drawing us closer through worship, reflection, and surrender to his healing process. Job's response shows that worship shifts our perspective from pain to God's faithfulness. Jesus's example shows that grief is a divine invitation to experience God's compassion, and Samson's story warns us of the dangers of unchecked sorrow. Through it all, we learn to depend not on ourselves but on God's power to redeem and restore us.

Finding God in Our Tears: Biblical Assurance

Grief, as depicted throughout Scripture, is not only acknowledged but also treated as an integral part of the human experience. The Bible provides numerous examples of individuals grappling with deep sorrow, assuring us that God fully understands and meets us in our pain. In many of these accounts, grief becomes a catalyst for a spiritual encounter, leading to transformation, healing, and even new beginnings. The narrative of grief is interwoven into the biblical story, showing us that while sorrow is inevitable, it is never without purpose.

In chapter 2, we explored the profound lessons found in Jonah's story, where unresolved emotions like anger and bitterness held him back from fulfilling God's ultimate calling. Jonah's reluctance to let go of his grief over Nineveh's impending redemption exemplifies how clinging to anger and bitterness can block the flow of God's grace. Jonah's refusal to forgive the Ninevites—a people he deemed unworthy—led to an internal struggle that mirrored his external journey away from God's will. As seen in Jonah 4:1–3, he was exceedingly angry over God's compassion toward Nineveh, illustrating that unresolved grief and anger can distort our perception of God's justice. Jonah's story serves as a sobering reminder that holding onto bitterness in times of grief obstructs the healing and peace God offers. However, when we release that bitterness, we invite God's transformative peace into our lives, allowing him to mend what is broken.

In contrast, Hezekiah's story from chapter 4 illustrates how grief, when coupled with fervent prayer, can sometimes lead to miraculous outcomes. Confronted with the news of his impending death, Hezekiah's response was to cry out to God in earnest prayer. Rather than causing him to turn inward or rebel against God's will, his grief drove him closer to God, seeking divine intervention (Isa 38:2–3). As a result, God granted him an additional fifteen years of life, demonstrating his responsiveness to heartfelt prayer. This narrative showcases that grief, when surrendered to God in prayer, can lead to both personal transformation and a tangible change in circumstances. Hezekiah's life is a testament to the power of prayer in the face of adversity, underscoring the truth of Ps 34:18, which assures us that "the Lord is close to the brokenhearted and saves those who are crushed in spirit." Through prayer, we engage with God more deeply, opening our hearts to his comfort and allowing his divine will to shape our reality.

This biblical framework for understanding grief underscores the duality of human emotion: while grief can drive us away from God (as seen with Jonah), it can also draw us nearer to him, as evidenced by Hezekiah's story. Jonah's bitter refusal to let go of his grief led to a heart hardened toward God's grace, preventing him from fully embracing his divine calling. This bitterness clouded his understanding of God's mercy, emphasizing that clinging to unresolved emotions can skew our perception of God's greater purpose for our lives. Conversely, Hezekiah's response to grief—by seeking God's intervention through prayer—led to life-altering results. These contrasting responses to grief teach us that the posture we take in moments of sorrow profoundly influences the trajectory of our spiritual journey.

Beyond these individual stories, the Bible offers additional insight into how God engages with those in mourning. Jesus, the very embodiment of divine compassion, wept openly at the death of Lazarus in John 11:35. His tears demonstrated that grief is not something to be dismissed or avoided; instead, it is an essential part of the human experience. By weeping alongside Lazarus's loved ones, Jesus affirmed the validity of their sorrow and provided divine empathy in their suffering. His tears reveal a God intimately familiar with our pain, a Savior who enters our grief and walks with us through it. This image of Jesus weeping communicates that, far from being distant in times of sorrow, God draws near, ready to provide comfort and healing to those who mourn.

In each of these biblical examples, the common thread is clear: grief becomes a space for divine encounter when we choose to surrender it to God. This divine encounter refers to the transformative experience of God's presence and grace in the midst of our sorrow. Whether through releasing bitterness, as Jonah struggled to do, or turning to God in prayer, as Hezekiah modeled, grief opens the door to deeper communion with God. In this way, the biblical stories of grief assure us that we are never alone in our sorrow. Psalm 34:18 offers a poignant reminder that God is "close to the brokenhearted and saves those who are crushed in spirit." His presence is not just near us; it is actively working to bring comfort, restoration, and new hope.

Key Insight

Engaging in prayer during grief has the potential to change not only our hearts but also the circumstances we face. Jonah's story is a cautionary tale about the dangers of holding onto unresolved anger and bitterness. In contrast, Hezekiah's story offers hope that through earnest prayer, God can bring about miraculous change even in the darkest times. Through it all, the Bible assures us that God is near to the brokenhearted, offering comfort, grace, and redemption to those who seek him. When we bring our grief before God, we open ourselves to his healing power, allowing him to transform our sorrow into something life giving. One practical way to engage with God during grief is to set aside specific times for prayer and reflection, allowing God to speak to us and comfort us in our pain.

Reflecting on these stories reminds us that while grief may seem overwhelming, it also provides a unique opportunity to encounter God's grace and mercy. Jonah and Hezekiah, though faced with different responses to grief, both illuminate the ways in which God works in the lives of the grieving. Jesus's tears at Lazarus's tomb further illustrate God's deep compassion for us in our pain, assuring us that our tears are sacred to him. In grief, God draws near, offering not only comfort but also the hope of transformation and redemption. Through prayer, worship, and surrender, we discover that God's presence in our grief is comforting and capable of changing our lives and circumstances. It is important to remember that we are not alone in our grief. The Christian community, through their love, support, and prayers, can also be a source of comfort and strength during these times.

The Hope Beyond Grief: Eternal Promises

As Christians, we are not left without hope when faced with grief. Though pain and loss are inescapable, our faith anchors us in the assurance that grief does not have the final word. The core of this hope is the resurrection of Christ, a powerful symbol of God's promise to restore, heal, and renew. This resurrection is more than a historical event; it is the foundation of our hope, demonstrating that even in death, there is a pathway to life.

In chapter 5, we encounter one of the most profound moments in the New Testament: Jesus's tears at the tomb of Lazarus.

These tears reveal something extraordinary—not because they anticipate Lazarus's resurrection, but because they display the heart of God toward humanity. Jesus, aware that he would bring Lazarus back to life, still chose to weep, entering deeply into the sorrow of those around him. His tears signify that God is not indifferent to our suffering; instead, he shares in our pain, underscoring that grief, while painful, is met with divine empathy.

The hope found in Jesus's weeping goes beyond an immediate escape from sorrow; it points us toward a larger truth: God is with us in our grief, and his response is always one of hope. Jesus's tears remind us that God is deeply engaged in the human experience of loss. Rather than rushing us past our sorrow, he joins us in it, offering comfort, compassion, and the assurance of his abiding presence.

The resurrection of Christ transforms our grief from despair to hope. This central truth teaches us that suffering, while real, is not eternal. Death—whether it is the loss of a loved one, the end of a chapter in life, or the breaking of a relationship—does not have the last word. God's ultimate renewal is the final word. As Paul writes in 1 Cor 15:54, "Death has been swallowed up in victory," emphasizing the promise of eternal life and the eventual restoration of all things.

This promise of renewal reshapes how we experience grief today. We mourn, but we do not mourn as those who have no hope (1 Thess 4:13). Our tears are infused with the knowledge that God is actively "making all things new" (Rev 21:5), reframing sorrow as a place of hopeful anticipation. We believe that God's restorative power works not only in eternity but also in our present struggles.

In this journey, grief becomes an opportunity to encounter God's grace in a deeper way. The resurrection assures us that God is actively working to heal and restore, even amid our pain, promising that every tear will one day be wiped away and that hope persists beyond even the darkest valleys. As we live between grief and hope, we are invited to embrace the certainty of God's eternal promises, knowing that our pain will not endure forever.

Key Insight

The resurrection of Christ transforms our grief, offering a promise that God's renewal is constantly at work, even in life's darkest moments. Jesus's tears at Lazarus's tomb reveal God's compassionate heart, while the resurrection points us to a transcendent hope, assuring us of God's ultimate victory over all sorrow.

Living Out the Lessons of Grief: Community and Support

Throughout our journey, we've learned that community plays an essential role in helping individuals navigate grief. Biblical examples reinforce this truth: Hezekiah's reliance on communal prayer in chapter 4 and Job's engagement with his friends in chapter 1 highlight that we are not meant to walk through grief alone. The community provides a vital support system that strengthens us when our own strength falters, offering comfort and encouragement through the presence of others who share our faith and empathize with our suffering.

In *Life Together*, Dietrich Bonhoeffer underscores the power of Christian fellowship, especially in times of hardship, asserting that "the Christian needs another Christian who speaks God's Word to him."[1] Bonhoeffer emphasizes that a Christian community reflects God's love and compassion, making his presence more palpable to those experiencing pain and loss.

The role of community is not simply to provide companionship; it is an extension of God's care, a means by which believers can encounter God's presence in tangible ways. Bonhoeffer suggests that being present with others in grief allows us to be conduits of divine comfort, helping others experience God's love through human connection.[2]

Additionally, research in psychology aligns with these theological insights, affirming that social support is crucial for

---

1. Bonhoeffer, *Life Together*, 47.
2. Bonhoeffer, *Life Together*, 47.

emotional healing and resilience during times of grief. Psychologist Sheryl Ziegler explains that "social isolation often exacerbates mental and emotional strain," highlighting how supportive relationships during difficult times can help reduce feelings of isolation and provide emotional regulation, which significantly aids the grieving process.[3] Studies show that individuals with access to robust social networks tend to experience fewer long-term negative effects from traumatic events. Social connections can decrease isolation, increase emotional resilience, and even mitigate stress responses, which is especially important during periods of intense mourning.

Scripture also offers insights into the importance of communal support. In Gal 6:2 Paul urges believers to "carry each other's burdens, and in this way you will fulfill the law of Christ." This biblical directive reflects God's vision of a supportive, interconnected community that mirrors his compassion and grace. Jesus demonstrated this relational model throughout his ministry, often sharing in others' suffering and grief, such as when he wept with Mary and Martha at the tomb of Lazarus. His actions illustrate that human connection in moments of sorrow is not only comforting but also divinely inspired. By following this model, Christian communities can embody God's love, helping each other find strength in faith.

Furthermore, the role of the community during grief is seen throughout history in the practices of the early church, which Bonhoeffer also admired. The early Christian communities frequently gathered to support one another in prayer and encouragement, especially in times of persecution and loss. This historical example serves as a powerful reminder of the enduring role of faith communities, not just as places of worship but as spaces of healing and solidarity.

Grief, therefore, becomes not an isolated experience but a shared journey within the body of Christ. The church can act as a family, bearing witness to one another's suffering and reminding each member of the hope and comfort found in God. In community,

---

3. Ziegler, *Mommy Burnout*, 25.

our individual sorrows are transformed, reminding us that we are never alone, as others share in our burdens and uplift us in prayer.

Conclusion: Embracing the Journey with Hope

Grief is a profound and universal experience that brings us face-to-face with the fragility of life and the depth of our emotional bonds. In the Christian faith, grief is not merely a passage through sorrow but a sacred journey that calls us to a deeper reliance on God, where sorrow becomes a space for divine encounter. Though it brings with it pain, grief invites us into transformative faith, urging us to lean on God's promises and embrace the comfort found in his unwavering presence. As we walk through valleys shadowed by loss, our grief is gradually transformed, not erased, into a powerful reminder of God's faithfulness.

Throughout Scripture, we find that grief and suffering do not alienate us from God; instead, they draw us nearer to him. Job's story, for instance, is often seen as a testament to resilience amid trials. Job's unwavering faith through immense suffering shows us that grief can be a space for encountering God's presence in a new way, even when we do not understand the reason behind our pain. Job's ultimate restoration (Job 42:10) emphasizes that while suffering may challenge our understanding of God's ways, it also gives us a renewed sense of his compassion and care. Job's experience speaks to the belief that our faith is not diminished by grief; instead, it is refined, teaching us to trust God's sovereignty even amid our sorrow.[4]

In Hezekiah's story, we are reminded of the power of prayer as a response to grief. When Hezekiah received the devastating news of his impending death, he turned immediately to prayer, and his heartfelt pleas were met with an extension of life (2 Kgs 20:1–6). This narrative illustrates the importance of bringing our grief to God, knowing he hears and responds to the prayers of those who call upon him earnestly. Through prayer, we are assured that God

---

4. Miller and Yamamori, *Global Pentecostalism*, 88.

is not a distant observer of our pain but an active participant in our healing. As Dietrich Bonhoeffer writes in *Life Together*, "God's Word in Jesus Christ pronounces us guilty, and His Word is a two-edged sword,"[5] reminding us that the sharpness of grief is always met with God's restorative presence.

Furthermore, grief, according to Christian thought, is not without hope. The resurrection of Christ lies at the core of this hope, serving as a powerful affirmation that death and suffering do not have the final word. The resurrection is not merely a historical event but a transformative promise that, in God's hands, even the most painful experiences can lead to new life and renewal.[6] This central Christian belief transforms grief from a final endpoint into a bridge toward eternal life and renewal. Paul's words in 1 Cor 15:54—"Death has been swallowed up in victory"—serve as a triumphant reminder that the sorrow of grief is temporary, destined to be replaced by joy in God's promised restoration.

As Christians, we are encouraged to confront grief with a "living hope," as described in 1 Pet 1:3, a hope rooted in Christ's resurrection. This hope does not deny the reality of our sorrow; instead, it allows us to live with the assurance that God's redemption is both present and future. We do not grieve as those "who have no hope" (1 Thess 4:13), for we know that our tears will ultimately be wiped away. Our pain will be redeemed in God's perfect time (Rev 21:4). Bonhoeffer's reflections on Christian fellowship affirm that God often meets us in our grief through the love and support of others, demonstrating his empathy and compassion through human connections. In this context, community becomes a testament to God's enduring presence among his people.

Grief also has the power to deepen our understanding of divine love. Jesus's tears at Lazarus's tomb serve as a profound example of God's empathy toward human suffering. In choosing to weep with Mary and Martha, Jesus reveals a God who does not stand detached from our sorrow but enters fully into our pain (John 11:35). This moment underscores that grief, while painful,

---

5. Bonhoeffer, *Life Together*, 47.
6. Wright, *Surprised by Hope*, 233.

can draw us closer to God's heart, as it is here that we encounter a God who deeply understands and shares in our suffering.[7] Jesus's willingness to share in human grief reaffirms that God's presence does not simply alleviate our pain but transforms it, giving our sorrow new meaning and purpose.

As the body of Christ, the church is called to embody this divine empathy, becoming a community where each person's grief is acknowledged and shared. Paul's exhortation in Gal 6:2, "Carry each other's burdens, and in this way you will fulfill the law of Christ," reminds us that we are not meant to bear our sorrow alone. The early church provides a historical model of this communal support, as believers gathered to encourage one another through prayer and solidarity, especially in times of hardship and persecution (Acts 2:42–47). In community, we are reminded that God's love is made tangible through the presence and care of others.

Ultimately, embracing grief as part of our faith journey allows us to see our suffering as part of God's redemptive work. In grief, we encounter a profound call to trust God's promises and to live in the hope of resurrection, knowing that our pain will be transformed. Grief, therefore, is not simply something to endure; it is an opportunity to deepen our reliance on God's grace, allowing his promises to sustain us through every trial. As we move through seasons of sorrow, we do so with the confidence that God walks with us, leading us toward the joy and renewal that await beyond the tears.

Application

Invite God into Your Grief

Start by acknowledging your pain and inviting God into your grieving process. Recognize that it's okay to feel sorrow, anger, or confusion. Trust that God is present with you, offering comfort, understanding, and healing in your moments of vulnerability. Pray and meditate, allowing his presence to provide solace and strength.

---

7. Brown, *Gospel According to John*, 172.

Practice Open Communication

Foster a habit of sharing your emotions openly with God and trusted individuals in your life. This openness cultivates connection and understanding, allowing you to express your feelings without fear of judgment. Writing in a journal can also help articulate your thoughts and emotions, deepening your relationship with God and those around you.

Seek Support

Lean on your community—friends, family, or support groups—during difficult times. Sharing your burdens with others can lighten the load and provide emotional support. Engaging with those who understand or have experienced similar losses can create a safe space for healing and encourage mutual support in faith.

Remember God's Promises

Hold fast to the promises of God, particularly the hope of eternal life and restoration. Reflect on scriptures that affirm God's faithfulness, such as 2 Cor 1:3-4, which speaks of God as "the Father of compassion and the God of all comfort." Let these promises sustain you through grief, reminding you that your sorrow is temporary and that joy will come.

Reflection Questions

1. How have I experienced God's presence in my grief?
2. How can I be more open about my emotions with God and others?
3. How can I support those around me in their grief?
4. What promises from Scripture give me hope as I navigate loss?

Closing Prayer

Heavenly Father, we come before you with hearts that carry the weight of grief and loss. We thank you for being a God who meets us in our tears, walking alongside us through every season of life. Help us to embrace our grief, recognizing it not as a sign of weakness but as an opportunity for a deeper connection with you. Teach us to open our hearts and invite you into our pain, trusting in your promise to heal and comfort us.

Lord, grant us the courage to share our burdens with others and to seek support from our community, knowing that we are not alone in this journey. May our sorrow draw us closer to you, reminding us that your grace is sufficient in our weakness. As we navigate this path, may our eyes remain fixed on the hope we have in Christ, who offers us eternal life and renewal beyond our understanding.

Help us to reflect on the love and comfort you provide, and may our journey through grief lead us to a deeper reliance on your unfailing grace. In Jesus's name, we pray. Amen.

About the Author

DR. MEL OQUENDO IS a dynamic ordained minister, chaplain, and passionate leader with over twenty-five years of experience in pastoral ministry. Having pastored both English- and Spanish-speaking congregations, Mel has successfully navigated diverse communities across Kissimmee, Florida; Orlando, Florida; Branson, Missouri; and Chicago, Illinois. His ministry transcends cultural boundaries, providing him with profound insights into the challenges believers face across multicultural and cross-cultural contexts.

As a sought-after speaker, lecturer, and mentor, Dr. Oquendo is regularly invited to conferences and workshops, speaking to leaders in diverse denominational settings. His expertise in multicultural leadership, pastoring, and marriage equips church leaders with the practical and theological tools they need to lead with excellence and compassion.

Mel's commitment to family is at the heart of his ministry. A devoted husband to Jeanette, a proud father of four children—Soniely, Junior, Arianna, and Joshua—and a grandfather to his precious granddaughter, Lehlani, his family continues to inspire and motivate him. Their love and support drive his passion for creating spaces where others can encounter God's transformative love and grace.

Dr. Oquendo holds a BS in ministerial leadership with a minor in pastoral leadership from Southeastern University, and an MDiv and DMin in preaching and leading from Asbury Theological Seminary. He serves as an adjunct professor and contributes

ABOUT THE AUTHOR

to academic roles with multiple institutions. Through his ministry, teaching, and conferences, Dr. Oquendo inspires individuals to embrace hope through life's challenges, encouraging spiritual growth even in the midst of adversity.

Bibliography

Augustine. *The City of God*. Carol Stream, IL: Tyndale House, 2009.
Billings, J. Todd. *Rejoicing in Lament: Wrestling with Incurable Cancer and Life in Christ*. Grand Rapids: Brazos, 2015.
Bock, Darrell L., with Benjamin I Simpson. *Jesus According to Scripture: Restoring the Portrait from the Gospels*. 2nd ed. Grand Rapids: Baker Academic, 2021.
Bonhoeffer, Dietrich. *Life Together: The Classic Exploration of Christian Community*. Translated by John W. Doberstein. San Francisco: HarperOne, 2009.
Bradshaw, John. *Healing the Shame That Binds You*. Updated ed. Deerfield Beach, FL: Health Communications, 2005.
Brown, Raymond E. *The Gospel According to John: XIII–XXI*. Anchor Yale Bible Commentaries. New Haven: Yale University Press, 1970.
Brueggemann, Walter. *The Message of the Psalms: A Theological Commentary*. Minneapolis: Augsburg, 1984.
Chester, Tim. *You Can Change: God's Transforming Power for Our Sinful Behavior and Negative Emotions*. Wheaton, IL: Crossway, 2010.
Coogan, Michael D. *The Old Testament: A Historical and Literary Introduction to the Hebrew Scriptures*. 3rd ed. New York: Oxford University Press, 2013.
Cooper, Burton Z. *Why God?* Atlanta: John Knox, 1988.
Created to Worship. "Yiye Avila—Testimonio Asesinato de Su Hija Carmen Ilia Avila." YouTube, Nov. 4, 2015. https://www.youtube.com/watch?v=71A23aESChc.
Dorsey, David A. *The Literary Structure of the Old Testament: A Commentary on Genesis–Malachi*. Grand Rapids: Baker Academic, 1999.
Dutton, Donald G. *The Domestic Assault of Women: Psychological and Criminal Justice Perspectives*. Vancouver, Can.: UBC Press, 1995.
Enright, Robert D. *Forgiveness Is a Choice: A Step-by-Step Process for Resolving Anger and Restoring Hope*. Washington DC: APA LifeTools, 2001.
Foster, Richard J. *Celebration of Discipline: The Path to Spiritual Growth*. San Francisco: HarperOne, 1998.
———. *Prayer: Finding the Heart's True Home*. San Francisco: HarperOne, 1992.

BIBLIOGRAPHY

Garbarino, James. *Lost Boys: Why Our Sons Turn Violent and How We Can Save Them.* New York: Free Press, 1999.

Gottman, John, and Joan DeClaire. *The Relationship Cure: A Five-Step Guide to Strengthening Your Marriage, Family, and Friendships.* New York: Crown, 2001.

Gottwald, Norman K. *The Tribes of Yahweh: A Sociology of the Religion of Liberated Israel, 1250–1050 BCE.* Maryknoll, NY: Orbis, 2002.

Grayson, A. Kirk. *From Tiglath-Pileser I to Ashur-nasir-apli II.* Vol. 2 of *Assyrian Royal Inscriptions.* Leuven, Belg.: Peeters, 1976.

Greig, Pete. *God on Mute: Engaging the Silence of Unanswered Prayer.* Grand Rapids: Zondervan, 2007.

Guthrie, Nancy. *Hearing Jesus Speak into Your Sorrow.* Carol Stream, IL: Tyndale House, 2009.

Hazeldine, Stuart, dir. *The Shack.* Santa Monica, CA: Summit Entertainment, 2017.

Herman, Judith Lewis. *Trauma and Recovery: The Aftermath of Violence—From Domestic Abuse to Political Terror.* New York: Basic, 1997.

James, John W., and Russell Friedman. *The Grief Recovery Handbook: The Action Program for Moving Beyond Death, Divorce, and Other Losses.* New York: HarperCollins, 2015.

Keener, Craig S. *The Gospel of John: A Commentary.* 2 volumes. Peabody, MA: Hendrickson, 2003.

Keller, Timothy. *Prayer: Experiencing Awe and Intimacy with God.* New York: Viking, 2014.

Koenig, Harold G. *Spirituality in Patient Care: Why, How, When, and What.* 3rd ed. West Conshohocken, PA: Templeton, 2013.

Kübler-Ross, Elisabeth, and David Kessler. *On Grief and Grieving: Finding the Meaning of Grief Through the Five Stages of Loss.* New York: Scribner, 2014.

Kushner, Harold S. *When Bad Things Happen to Good People.* New York: Schocken, 1981.

Lewis, C. S. *A Grief Observed.* San Francisco: HarperOne, 2001.

———. *The Problem of Pain.* San Francisco: HarperOne, 2001.

Luskin, Fred. *Forgive for Good: A Proven Prescription for Health and Happiness.* New York: Morrow, 2007.

Mayo Clinic. "Hydrocephalus." Sept. 15, 2023. https://www.mayoclinic.org/diseases-conditions/hydrocephalus/symptoms-causes/syc-20373604.

McCormack, Jerusha Hull. *Grieving: A Beginner's Guide.* Downers Grove, IL: InterVarsity, 2016.

Miller, Donald E., and Tetsunao Yamamori. *Global Pentecostalism: The New Face of Christian Social Engagement.* Berkeley: University of California Press, 2007.

Moltmann, Jürgen. *The Crucified God: The Cross of Christ as the Foundation and Criticism of Christian Theology.* Minneapolis: Fortress, 1993.

Morris, Leon. *The Gospel According to John.* Rev. ed. New International Commentary on the New Testament. Grand Rapids: Eerdmans, 2008.

BIBLIOGRAPHY

Nouwen, Henri J. M. *The Wounded Healer: Ministry in Contemporary Society*. New York: Doubleday, 1979.

Nussbaum, Martha C. *The Fragility of Goodness: Luck and Ethics in Greek Tragedy and Philosophy*. Rev. ed. Cambridge: Cambridge University Press, 2008.

Orloff, Judith. *Emotional Freedom: Liberate Yourself from Negative Emotions and Transform Your Life*. New York: Three Rivers, 2010.

Packer, J. I. *Knowing God*. Downers Grove, IL: InterVarsity, 1973.

Pargament, Kenneth I. *The Psychology of Religion and Coping: Theory, Research, Practice*. New York: Guilford, 1997.

Piper, John. *Desiring God: Meditations of a Christian Hedonist*. Colorado Springs: Multnomah, 2003.

Smedes, Lewis B. *The Art of Forgiving: When You Need to Forgive and Don't Know How*. New York: Ballantine, 1996.

Sproul, R. C. *Chosen by God*. Wheaton, IL: Tyndale House, 1986.

Tozer, A. W. *The Knowledge of the Holy*. San Francisco: HarperOne, 1961.

Vingerhoets, Ad. *Why Only Humans Weep: Unravelling the Mysteries of Tears*. Oxford: Oxford University Press, 2013.

Volf, Miroslav. *Exclusion and Embrace: A Theological Exploration of Identity, Otherness, and Reconciliation*. Nashville: Abingdon, 1996.

Vroegop, Mark. *Dark Clouds, Deep Mercy: Discovering the Grace of Lament*. Wheaton, IL: Crossway, 2019.

Walton, John H. *Job*. NIV Application Commentary. Grand Rapids: Zondervan, 2014.

———. *Jonah: A Bible Study Commentary*. Grand Rapids: Zondervan, 1982.

Walton, John H., et al. *The IVP Bible Background Commentary: Old Testament*. Downers Grove, IL: InterVarsity, 2000.

Westberg, Granger E. *Good Grief*. Minneapolis: Fortress, 2011.

Wiersbe, Warren W. *Real Worship: Playground, Battle Ground, or Holy Ground?* 2nd ed. Grand Rapids: Baker, 2000.

Willard, Dallas. *The Divine Conspiracy: Rediscovering Our Hidden Life in God*. 20th anniv. ed. New York: HarperOne, 2018.

———. *Renovation of the Heart: Putting on the Character of Christ*. 10th anniv. ed. Colorado Springs: NavPress, 2012.

Wolfelt, Alan D. *The Journey Through Grief: Reflections on Healing*. Fort Collins, CO: Companion, 2003.

Wolterstorff, Nicholas. *Lament for a Son*. Grand Rapids: Eerdmans, 1987.

Wright, H. Norman. *The Complete Guide to Crisis & Trauma Counseling: What to Do and Say When It Matters Most!* Minneapolis: Bethany House, 2011.

Wright, N. T. *The Crown and the Fire: Meditations on the Cross and the Life of the Spirit*. San Francisco: HarperOne, 2016.

———. *Evil and the Justice of God*. Downers Grove, IL: InterVarsity, 2014.

———. *The Resurrection of the Son of God*. Christian Origins and the Question of God 3. Minneapolis: Fortress, 2008.

BIBLIOGRAPHY

———. *Simply Jesus: A New Vision of Who He Was, What He Did, and Why He Matters.* San Francisco: HarperOne, 2011.

———. *Surprised by Hope: Rethinking Heaven, the Resurrection, and the Mission of the Church.* San Francisco: HarperOne, 2008.

Yancey, Philip. *Where Is God When It Hurts?* Grand Rapids: Zondervan, 1997.

Ziegler, Sheryl. *Mommy Burnout: How to Reclaim Your Life and Raise Healthier Children in the Process.* New York: Dey St., 2018.